'TAILWINDS & TEAPOTS'

My life as a BOAC steward in the 1970s

Robert Thornton

I dedicate this to book my long-suffering wife Susan, who puts up with me on a daily basis. Without her patience and support throughout the writing of this book it would never have seen the light of day!

CONTENTS

INTRODUCTION

These ramblings cover the years I spent flying as cabin crew for BOAC in the early 1970s. My days flying as a steward were among the best working days of my life. It was a demanding job; and definitely not just about serving drinks and meals to passengers. To the outsider it looked a glamourous way of life. Yet, in reality, it was an extraordinary and dislocated lifestyle, unlike anything in civvy street. We travelled the world, but odd hours, jet-lag, extreme climates, and long periods away from home, were the norm. That said, it was great fun and that made up for any hardship.

Many of the flights I worked on did not conform to the published timetable of the day. This was, in part, due to the oil crisis in the run up to the 1973 Arab Israeli war. At the time, oil supplies were a major headache for airlines. Simply put, supplies did not match demand. The impact this had on crews took the form of cancelled services and last-minute roster changes. As a result, we could leave London on one roster and end up flying to completely different places than those we were originally scheduled to visit. A five-day trip could easily turn into three weeks without warning.

The 1970s was the era of the Ford Cortina, Raleigh Chopper bikes, record players, and cassette recorders. It was a decade of strikes and the height of street battles and sectarian killings in Northern Ireland. Pounds, shillings, and pence went decimal. Britain joined the Common Market. Rolls Royce went bust and was nationalised. Platform shoes, flared trousers, dodgy hairdos, and hot pants were the fashion of the time, and the world's first Hard Rock Café opened in London. Barbie, Sindy, and Action Man were the top toys and 'Get It On' by T-Rex was riding high in the charts. Home computers were a decade away. People rented their tellies by the month from Rediffusion. The average price of a house was £5000 and the inflation rate in the UK was 8.6%.

On the global stage, Tricky Dickie was the US president, and Brezhnev, his Russian counterpart. The Khmer Rouge genocide in Cambodia was becoming a reality, Idi Amin seized power in Uganda, and five hundred thousand people marched in Washington DC protesting against the Vietnam War. Starbucks was yet to open its first coffee shop!

In space, Apollo's 14 and 15 land on the moon. Russia successfully launches the world's first manned space station, Salyut 1, and becomes the first country to land a spacecraft on the surface of Mars.

In the air, 'The Golden Age of Air Travel' was drawing to a close. The introduction of the Jumbo jet in 1969 heralded in the age of mass tourism and with it came an ability to connect continents and shrink the world. The era of 'cattle class' had arrived!

Gone were the days when Middle East princes gave crews Rolex watches as a thank-you gift. Concorde was yet to enter commercial passenger service. Flight deck doors weren't locked, and airport security was virtually non-existent - making hijacking of aircraft the preferred modus operandi for any would-be terrorist!

Thus the stage is set!

'There was no hint of what was about to unfold'.
(Dan Clark Collection)

1. TESTING TIMES

'Part of The Union'

The Strawbs

*'Above your head are the control buttons
for your reading light and the flight
attendant call button. The reading
light button will switch your light on
and off. Yet, no matter how many
times you push the other one it will
not turn on your flight attendants.'*

I left the draconian environment of boarding school, with its overbearing teachers and mud-ridden cross-country runs, at sixteen. I flirted with a life treading the boards, appearing in London at the Barbican and Shaw Theatre but soon realised an actor's life wasn't for me! Instead, I went to work for an insurance company in the City of London. From the sublime to the ridiculous; or was it the other way around? Either way, I was to prove ill-matched to this line of work! My job was that of a tax clerk which involved endless days filling out other people's annual tax returns. For this I earned the enormous sum of ten pounds a week! I lasted about a year before leaving and moving to a firm of chartered accountants off Cavendish Square - money being my motivation. This too was a poor career choice. From the minute I arrived, I hated the place. I toughed it out for a year before getting yet another job as a tax clerk, this time in provincial Epsom. Was there no limit to my stupidity? John Cleese had the right idea about chartered accountancy; it was the living death of Monty Python fame!

I saw my chance of escape when I came across a newspaper ad promising a glamorous jet set life living in first-class hotels in exotic locations. The world of BOAC beckoned. And all for a lot more money than I was earning in Epsom. Accountancy lost and I applied to go flying. It was no contest because: I had always wanted to travel and see the world, I hated my job, I didn't want to join the Navy, roughing it on the hippie trail didn't appeal, and I didn't want to be a lumberjack!

The element of theatre about the job also appealed to me as I saw certain similarities between being a steward and being an actor. The crew are the cast, giving a performance; passengers their audience.

The show may have only been staged in a narrow aisle, but it was a show nevertheless!

And finally, the notion occurred to me that I might stumble upon a more adventurous way of life in some far-flung corner of the world. This thought was prompted by something an accountancy colleague volunteered. He reckoned I would end up as a drug dealer in Port Said! Not that I wanted to be a drug dealer, but something else in Port Said? Although he was to be proved wrong, flying did open a door to a far more interesting life than one promised by tax forms.

BOAC (British Overseas Airways Corporation) was, at the time, the UK's state-owned national airline operating long-haul services across the globe out of Heathrow. The other major UK airlines were BEA (British European Airways), BCal (British Caledonian), and Dan-Air.

BEA operated short-haul flights within Europe from Heathrow, whereas BCal were almost entirely based at Gatwick so weren't considered a rival to BOAC. And then there was Dan Scare. Enough said!

My first ever experience of flying was with BEA. This was on a Vickers Viscount from London to Basel, where our family lived. I don't know exactly how old I was, I must have been around eight or nine, but I loved it. By modern standards, with forty passengers flying at an altitude of twenty-five thousand feet, it was rudimentary. By the standards of the time, it was a technological marvel. To me, the sound of the Rolls Royce propeller engines rejoicing in my ears was awesome. For most of the flight, it was bumpy, which didn't bother me at all. What I remember most was the postcard the steward gave me as a souvenier. To me it was a treasure. Did this simple act start me on the path toward becoming a steward myself? I like to think so.

There was a good-natured rivalry between BOAC and BEA. In reality, there was little rivalry as BEA had the European market and we had the long-haul sector.

BOAC crews said BEA stood for Back Each Afternoon, as they more or less only did day trips. Another was Better Eat Afterwards.

But BOAC also had to take it as well as dish it out. To our rivals, our initials stood for: Better On A Camel, Bringing Over American Cash, Boy's Overseas After Crumpet, and/or Blast Off And Crash! And then there was Bend Over Again, Christine! This one came about as a result of the Profumo affair in the early 1960s. John Profumo, Secretary of State for War in Macmillan's government, was sleeping with Christine Keeler, a 19-year-old 'would-be model', who also shared her bed with the Russian naval attaché at the time. The resulting scandal shook the political establishment to the core as it was thought Profumo may be unwittingly giving away secrets to the Russians in his pillow talk with Keeler – who then passed it on in her pillow talk with the naval attaché. I can only assume Profumo used to fly BOAC, which would make sense as he was a government minister.

To be fair, most of the world's airlines were given names, here are a few examples:

AIR FRANCE: Air Chance.

ALITALIA: Always Late In Taking-off, Always Late In Arriving.

KLM: Kinky Leather Merchants.

MEA: Moth Eaten Airline.

PAN AM: Passengers Always Neglected At Mealtimes.

PIA: Please Inform Allah.

QANTAS: Quite A Nice Trip, Any Survivors? Quick And Nasty Typical Australian Service.

SABENA: Such A Bad Experience Never Again.

SAS: Sex and Satisfaction! Sweet and Sexy.

SINGAPORE INTERNATIONAL AIRLINES: Sex In The Air.

TWA: Try Walking Across. Tinnie Winnie

Airline. That Was Awful.

I have left out what we called Lufthansa on the grounds of decency, as well as some of the other things Pan Am and Qantas got called!

An aircrew job with BOAC, because of its global nature, was a sought-after prize. As a result, competition to 'land' a job with them was intense.

In applying for the job, I had to fulfil the following criteria:

Aged between 20 – 26

Excellent health and eyesight

Smartness of dress, clear skin and a good bearing

Height between 5'6" and 6' 2", weight between 126 and 180 lbs.

Pleasant personality and good speaking voice

Responsible and enthusiastic approach to work

Education standard needs to be to at least O level

British national with a British passport

Conversational ability in West European language (other than English)

Experience of working or looking after people

For the girls they also had to have a 'neatly-proportioned figure', with recruiters favouring girls who had a shapely pair of legs! They also had to be single. If they got married at any time after they joined the airline, they had to leave!

How I got the job remains a mystery to me, given competition was fierce. Only one applicant in two hundred made it into training school. True, I satisfied the first eight criteria, but came nowhere on the last two! The fact that I made it at all was nothing short of remarkable!

My success may have been down to three things. First, I was in the Territorial Army, now the Army Reserves. The fact I was a soldier with the Royal Signals would have added brownie points to my application. Second, I had gone to a good boarding school. The Royal Russell School, whose patron was the Queen, had a good reputation and a posh school never harmed anyone's chances! Third, I was always ready to take the lead in something. Here's what I mean.

Before the interview, we had to wait together in a large room to be summonsed for our individual interviews. Not an extrovert by nature, I had learned the art of appearing to be more outgoing than I was at school - a necessary survival mechanism! With everyone in the room silently sitting waiting for something to happen, I took the initiative and started chatting with some of my fellow candidates around the room. It felt like the right thing to do. It occurred to me sometime later that one of the 'applicants' may have been a member of the interviewing team observing people's behaviour. If that were true, I must have gained some more brownie points for my loud mouth!

When I got the job, my mother greeted the news with her usual disapproval. '*A glorified flying waiter*', was her derogatory verdict on it. She would have been happier if I had landed a job at the post office or at a building society. Nine to five office jobs she understood - unlike the irregular hours of aviation. The fact that I had beaten one hundred and ninety-nine other people to the post was, sadly, lost on her. I was on an audit in a potato seed merchants counting bags of seeds (it doesn't get more glamourous than that!) when the letter came through with my joining details. I was to start the following week. To their credit, my employers let me off my notice and I was free to start as requested. Truth be told, they were probably glad to be rid of me! I have to admit, I wasn't much good at tax work! I suspect this is why they employed me to count potato seeds as far from the office as possible! It turned out I got a lot of notice over the start date! Some recruits received their letter on the day they were supposed to start. And, in some cases, days after their course had begun!

The following week I reported to the BOAC Training Centre at Heathrow, Cranebank, ready for the six-week course. I had swopped annual tax returns, and a boss who dried his socks on the office radiator, for a world of adventure. Well, one where I pushed a trolley up and down the aisle of a plane!

Situated to the east of Heathrow, the centre was a modern state-of-the-art facility, a far cry from the dingy, cramped office I had just left. There were seventeen of us in the men's group, with a similar number of girls on a parallel course. In those days, the two sexes trained apart, except for a few shared modules. What did we need with hair and makeup? For our part, us boys were a bit of a motley crew with an assortment of backgrounds. There was a fellow escapee from accountancy, a butcher, a baker, a nurse, and a couple of shop assistants. Whilst we didn't have a candlestick maker, we did have a BEA steward swopping the grind of short haul for the glamour of long haul! Amazingly, there were some who had never flown before - their first flight would be as crew! Although we had very diverse jobs before joining, we all had two things in common. A desire to see the world, and an almighty ignorance of what we had let ourselves in for!

My digs were in Colnbrook, close to the airport. I shared a room with another guy, the only BOAC staff there. The other 'inmates' were from a variety of walks of life. Unfortunately, after only a short time living there, the landlady took against me. To this day, I honestly have no idea why. Maybe it had something to do with the fact that I encouraged her son to go out clubbing on week nights! I know, I should have been studying! Luckily, I only lodged there Monday to Friday, escaping at the weekends to go home. Four weeks into the course, on my return one Sunday evening, matters came to a head. No sooner had I got through the door, than the landlady accused me of blocking the toilet. Apparently, I had been shoving rolls of toilet paper down it. When I pointed out that it couldn't have been me, seeing how I'd been in Kent the whole weekend, this cut no ice. She had decided I was guilty. I decided she was mad! She even threatened to report me to BOAC and have me thrown off the course. So, seeing how she was barking mad, I just let her get on with it. True, she could have had me thrown out of the house, which would have reflected badly on me with my new employer, but a change of digs would hardly have been a punishment! In the end, she did nothing and I stayed the duration – but it was like living in a war zone those last weeks! Come to think of it, it was the perfect preparation for some of the places I was about to travel to!

The course itself comprised written work, complete with multiple choice tests, classroom lectures, and practical sessions. The tests were weekly and failure to pass resulted in getting booted off the course. To be fair to the instructors, they worked hard to get everyone through. The practical sessions were held in the cabin services mock-up, the local swimming pool, and the airport's fire burning ground, aka the airport's fire service training area.

We learned how to deploy escape slides, fight fires, heat and serve meals, mix cocktails, make coffee, write reports, manage money, and deliver babies! The mixing of cocktails was a mote point. We never mixed them in economy; all we had to know was what went into a particular cocktail and then give the passenger the correct ingredients and garnishes - they did the rest!

There was a whole heap of other stuff I couldn't

see the point of us knowing, particularly the principles of flight. It was interesting, but the relevance passed me by. I needed to know how to switch an oven on and brew a regulation cup of coffee, but knowing the physics behind what kept the plane in the air was definitely an academic exercise as far as I could work out. Unless we were ever called upon to fly the plane, I suppose!

Soft skills were not neglected either. We had sessions on personal grooming and how to smile at passengers! The 'smile' we learnt was more of a rictus grin, switched on automatically when leaving the galley! The girls also had make-up and deportment classes to master! It may have been from a different time when debutantes became air hostesses, but I had this vision of girls walking around with books on their head in the deportment class!

One day, while coming to grips with an escape slide for the first time, I managed to break it as I was removing it from its stowage. At the time, we were learning how to use the Standard VC10's escape slide located above the door, not at floor level. The phrase "Doors to manual" hadn't been invented! In an emergency, we had to remove the slide from the roof and lower it to the ground before attaching it to the door with a clip. Only then could the door be opened and the slide deployed. My first attempt was a disaster. It jammed and stuck fast. As none of the instructors could shift it, the training session ended prematurely. In my defense, the design of the whole contraption was wrong. No airplane designer has ever put a slide above a door since, for good reason. The problem was that every time I flew on a Standard VC10, I dreaded the idea of having to deploy the slide in a real emergency! Luckily for me, breaking the training equipment wasn't a reason for getting booted off the course!

Needless to say, we had to experience for ourselves what it was like to evacuate from a plane using the slides. We had to climb up a gantry platform, where the slides were hung from. From that perch, and on the command *"Jump and Sit"*, we had to launch ourselves down the slide. It was great fun. More like a fun fair thrill than the serious business of escaping a burning plane. However, to make sure we realised this wasn't a frivolous game, our trainers took us to look at one particular emergency exit door. The door came from the ill-fated Whiskey Echo.

Whiskey Echo was the call sign for a BOAC 707 that crashed in a fireball at Heathrow three years earlier. The plane suffered an engine failure on take-off which led to a catastrophic fire. Metal fatigue, the same cause of the Comet crashes in the early 1950s, was why the engine failed. The crew executed an emergency landing, but when the pilots applied reverse thrust to slow the plane down, this blew flames from the burning engine forward underneath the wing. As a result, the fuselage was engulfed in fire. As the fire intensified it ignited fuel lines and caused oxygen tanks to explode, allowing fire to penetrate into the cabin. Five people lost their lives in the crash.

That more people didn't die was testament to the bravery of the cabin crew, especially that of stewardess Barbara Jane Harrison. One of those to die in the crash, she was posthumously awarded the George Cross for her part in saving many of the passengers. She is one of only four women to receive the medal for heroism, and the only one in peacetime.

This hit home. It made me very aware of the potential risks that came with the role, and they were real. As were the responsibilities of the job. Being cabin crew wasn't, and isn't, just about serving food and drink. It's about being there in an emergency. Passengers may have taken little notice of us when we were serving them a meal, but they looked to us for salvation in an emergency.

Whiskey Echo wasn't the only 707 BOAC lost. In 1966, Flight 911 had crashed over Mount Fuji. All one hundred and thirteen passengers and eleven crew on board perished. The aircraft was on a round-the-world flight when the accident happened soon after take-off from Tokyo. The investigation into the crash concluded the tail fin disintegrated after the plane encountered severe turbulence above Mount Fuji. This resulted in the aircraft going into a flat spin, from which there was no recovery. Personally, I have my doubts over the wisdom of this verdict, as I believe the cause was more about recklessness on the part of the captain because he deviated from his planned route to take passengers on a sightseeing jolly over the volcano, despite previous reports from aircraft that day about severe turbluence over the mountain. One thing, however, was abundantly clear. Flying was a far riskier enterprise than tax accountancy ever could be!

With the horrors of Whiskey Echo fresh in our minds, the next bit of our course involved a visit to the fire burning ground where we had to learn how to fight fires and escape from a burning plane.

One of the things we had to do was go into a building that was filled with smoke. It was a maze-like structure that we had to find our way out of. The technique was to crouch down as low to the ground as possible and head for the exit - PDQ! There were no lights to help, the whole place was in near total darkness. Which, to be fair, would probably be the conditions we would have to deal with in an accident. Nowadays crew have smoke hoods for such eventualities; we just had to hold our breath! On our course, we only had one 'casualty'. A stewardess, overcome by the smoke, had to be dragged out by a fireman. The things folk will do to be slung over a fireman's shoulder! After that, we had to put out a fuel fire. A big trough was filled with jet fuel and the fire guys set it alight. The heat generated was unbelievable. It was an amazing demonstration of just how hot it would become inside a burning fuselage and how dreadful conditions must have been aboard Whiskey Echo that fateful day.

As well as playing with fire, we also got to play with water. This had nothing to do with putting fires out, but everything to do with surviving if the aircraft had to make an emergency landing on the sea! We did this at the local swimming pool, and it was hysterical.

On the serious side, we had to know what to do to survive in the event of the aircraft ditching, although I doubt the local municipal baths were a very good substitute for the North Atlantic in winter – or any ocean at any time of year for that matter!

We had to learn how to deploy and inflate life rafts, and master the art of getting into them from the water. As we were wearing life jackets, which obstructed our every move, this was easier said than done! Once we had deployed the life raft, we then had to get in the water and attempt to clamber into it. We didn't need to be able to swim to get the job, but as my room-mate discovered, it sure helped! Picture the scene. Those of us who could swim are happily splashing around in the pool, probably not taking things too seriously to be fair! And then there was my roommate - flat on his back, completely at the mercy of his jacket. As he drifted past me, arms and legs flailing around uselessly, all he wanted to know, and I quote, was "*How do I stop the effing thing*".

As a confident swimmer, I was one of the last to climb aboard. As I hauled myself in and was about to tumble onto the floor, the floor disappeared. More accurately, it sank! The floor had parted company with the sides of the raft, dumping everyone into the water. For my hapless roommate, this was pretty much the last straw. I was amazed he didn't give up there and then on becoming an airline steward! I'm told the first thing people involved in dealing with an emergency need to do is breathe. Well, I'm really not sure that would have helped. Holding my breath seemed to make more sense in this situation! Which was difficult as I couldn't stop laughing at the sight of all my course mates flailing around at their unexpected dunking! You had to see the funny side of it!

After we had untangled ourselves from the wreckage, and escaped to the safety of the side, our instructors took great delight in telling us that if that had been the North Atlantic in winter, we would have died in under three minutes from hyperthermia! I remember thinking, 'I hope the rafts on the planes are in better nick than this one!'

Just to make sure we got the message that we needed to be able to cope in an accident, the trainers made us watch some Canadian Air Force films that showed what happened inside a cabin in a plane crash. One of the films showed a plane in which passengers had been replaced by crash dummies to demonstrate what happened to passengers in the event of an accident. It wasn't pretty and was a whole lot more violent than I had expected. Well, it would be, I guess!

We also got to see what happened when a plane has a decompression, caused by a window blowing out or a hole appearing in the fuselage. When the decompression occurred, oxygen masks dropped down from the panels above the seats in order to stop passengers suffering hypoxia, oxygen starvation. (For some reason, none of the dummies put their masks on! They weren't called dummies for no good reason!) As the masks dropped, the plane filled with a dense white mist. This is caused by the sudden change in air temperature with ice cold air mixing with the warm air in the cabin. What the film couldn't show was how passengers would feel during this process. Terror aside, even with a mask on people can feel lightheaded because they

18

breathe too rapidly into the mask (understandable) and they experience the silence that immediately follows a decompression – as happens when a bomb detonates. And they would also experience the same ringing in their ears that comes when a bomb explodes close to you. Suitably briefed, if not totally reassured, all I could hope was that I would never have the pleasure.

****

Under the watchful eye of the indomitable Sister Gatty, inevitably nicknamed Sister Batty, we tackled the vexed subject of first aid, grandly called aviation medicine. This part of the course was mixed so, along with the female trainees, we practiced CPR, bandaging broken limbs, and dressing burns. We used a dummy to practice on and one thing was certain, the CPR dummy wasn't the only one in the room! We were all doing a pretty good impression along those lines! At the end of the session, the room resembled a 1930's Boris Karloff film set with bandaged zombies replacing trainee stewards and stewardesses.

There is, of course, a comedian in every class. I can't remember exactly what quips were bandied around on my course, but they would have been along the lines of this. Trainer: *"If someone is hyperventilating, get them to breathe into a brown paper bag.*" Student: "*Does it have to be brown?*" Personally, I told any passenger breathing too rapidly to use a cuspidor (sick bag). Worked just as well as a paper bag, of any colour, and they were ready for the worst if the remedy failed!

The more advanced techniques we tackled included injecting oranges with hypodermic needles and watching babies being delivered. On video that is, not for real! Apparently, this 'qualified' us to deliver a baby. God help the poor thing should we ever have tried!

Despite all this medical training, at the end of it I had the unshakeable feeling that any 'patient' of mine would do well to survive the encounter!

During this part of the course, we had to make various trips to visit the company doctor to get our vaccinations. Yellow fever, tetanus, cholera, and typhoid, to name but a few! A part of me did, at this point, question what I may have let myself in for. I had joined to travel and see the world, not to catch a terminal disease! And the doc's bedside manner was distincly lacking! He took a pragmatic, almost brutal approach, devoid of any bedside manner whatsoever! After pumping me full of deadly microbes in both arms I was told to go home, take two aspirin with a pint of water and retire to bed! Guess what? I survived the night, but had unbelievable stiff arms the following day! Little did I know then that these injections were to save my life a couple of years later.

There was also advice offered of a more down to earth, practical nature. Such as, how to cope with diarrhoea down the routes! Apparently, Delhi Belly came with the territory and we needed to be able to cope with it while we were away. So, our trainers passed on a simple remedy for dealing with the trots. This was to peel and grate an apple, sprinkle it with sugar, then leave it to go brown before eating. You then washed it down with as much flat lemonade as the stomach could take. It worked like a dream, every time! The sealing of a Pharaoh's tomb comes to mind! As all the ingredients were readily available in any crew hotel, it was a remedy we could use wherever we were in the world. However, despite its undoubted efficacy, I never left home without packing a bottle of the magic pink liquid that was Pepto Bismol!

Along with this advice, we were also given dire warnings about food hygiene standards down the routes, which could be poor in third world countries. There were some places, like the sampans in the Hong Kong typhoon shelters, where I would never eat. Anywhere that rinses dishes in the harbour, has rats running around the floor, and has a bucket as a toilet, was not for me! As a result of the lack of rudimentary hygiene standards in many cities, crews mostly ate in a few trusted haunts and the crew hotel.

Malaria was another problem! Here the preventative measures we were given were all but useless! When operating along malarious routes in East or West Africa, we were advised to take Lapudrine once a week, and Proguanil daily. The problem was we went in and out of malaria areas all the time, often only stopping there for twenty-four hours. If rostered to Africa on a 1½ hour standby trip, there wasn't the time for the tablets to work! A lot of crew, myself included, relied instead on spraying our hotel rooms with insecticide, and consuming lots of tonic water! The quinine in the tonic acted as a substitute for the anti-malaria tablets. Back in the day, quinine was prescribed to combat malaria, but it would take gallons of the stuff to be anywhere close to effective. As I don't recall anyone getting malaria, we must have drunk gallons – laced with alcohol of course!

****

Catering was a massive part of a steward's life, so it was always going to form a major part of the training.

BOAC prided itself on the quality of its meals and cabin service, a standard we were expected to uphold. As the airline decreed passengers needed to be fed every four hours, we had to master meal service routines for breakfast, lunch, afternoon tea, and dinner. Behind this requirement, lay a monster logitics operation - with an annual shopping list that included 120,000 chickens, 96,000 bottles of champagne, and 108,000 bottles of wine.

During the six weeks we must have become reasonably adept at delivering the level of service demanded. However, as this was only in the mock-up, where the floor didn't move and the 'passengers' were our course mates, I am not sure how competent we really were when we left training! Serving food and drinks to real passengers on a real plane, in turbulence, was clearly going to be challenging whatever the trainers said! Curiously, I have no memory of this part of the course, or being taught how to use the galley equipment. I must have done it because I knew how to do it when I got on the aircraft - it's just one of those black holes!

One thing I do recall was training to use the PA. For many of the course, the prospect of public speaking was daunting to say the least. The fear of making a fool of oneself was a real possibility. Fortunately for me, I had become used to speaking in public at an early age. By the time I was twelve, I was a veteran at reading the lesson in the local church and speaking at school assemblies. I have no idea how I got the church gig; it may have something to do with the fact I am told I have a slightly posh voice, but it did set me up for life in terms of public speaking and probably had some influence on my pathetic attempts on the London stage!

For the PA, it wasn't good enough just to stammer out a few vague announcements as we had to give passengers precise information, not rough approximations. Phrases like *"We will be flying at about 30,000 feet"*, had to be replaced with *"We will be flying at 30,000 feet"*. Or, *"Our flight time will be around six and a half hours"*, replaced with *"Our flight time will be six and a half hours!"*. I got it. Aviation, if it is anything, is a precise business!

But not all our training sessions were about our flight duties. For example, we picked up tips on the best way to pack a suitcase. The trick was to pack the case in two halves. Top half was for short trips, bottom half for long trips. This way we always had all the clothes we ever needed if the trip we were on changed after leaving Heathrow. Which was hardly an unknown occurrence! Virtually everyone bought the standard crew case, a Globetrotter, costing around £15.00. The case was a kind of badge of honour, proclaiming the owner as aircrew. I was as proud of my case as I was of my brevet (my wing).

We also had to suffer being harangued by the local union rep. In those days, BOAC was a closed shop;

meaning employers only hired union members. Accordingly, anyone flying for BOAC had to join a union. Like it or not. Brother George, as the rep called himself, together with his sidekick, were on a mission. To me they looked like a comedy version of Batman and Robin! Or possibly Stan and Ollie! Their role was to sign us up and objection wasn't an option. If we refused, we were told, we were off the course. So, we all dutifully signed on the dotted line because there was no alternative if we wanted the job. Amazingly, thirty years later the scene repeated itself when I joined BAA, the airport operator of Heathrow, among others. This time, another union double act appeared on my induction course! They told us we all had to join the union, or else. But times had moved on and this naked attempt to bully people into signing up was ill judged. Closed shops had been made illegal years before this. Unsurprisingly, I wasn't about to be meekly compliant in the way I had been when I was twenty. I refused to join. Emboldened by my stand, a number of other people took my lead and became refuseniks! From that day on I was never going to be a popular figure with the union!

Unions aside, after six weeks in the classroom and mock-ups, we had learnt all we needed to know to fly as crew. There was no great fanfare, I simply got my Cabin Services Diploma, wing and my one stripe, and a group photo for successfully surviving the ordeal! If nothing else, this proved we had coped with all the trainers could throw at us. Not since getting my first pair of long trousers, or receiving an Honours Certificate from the 'Coulsdon and Purley Music Festival', for my recorder playing, aged eleven, was I that pleased! I was now a qualified Second Steward. Little did I know then, but I would return to Cranebank within two years for my conversion course to 747s!

Class of June/July 1971 Passing Out Parade – I'm circled front row.

As a Second Steward, I had entered a fraternity with roots that went back to 1912 when Heinrich Kubis, a German waiter, became the world's first air steward looking after passengers aboard the Zeppelin LZ 10 Schwaben airship. The Schwaben carried just twenty-four passengers in a gondola slung under the airship's frame. Kubis also worked on the ill-fated Hindenburg when it was totally destroyed by fire which killed thirty-six people; he survived.

As for the girls, stewardesses didn't appear until 1930 when a twenty-five-old nurse called Ellen Church convinced United Airlines that it would be a good idea to have someone looking after passengers who had the benefit of medical training. Whilst Kubis had begun the tradition associated with in-flight service, Church introduced the concept behind aviation medicine as we know it today.

Nelly Diener was the first woman to become a stewardess in Europe when Swissair gave her the job in 1934. Sadly, she was killed in the July 1934 Swissair Tuttlingen accident.

One of BOAC's predecessors, Imperial Airways, employed 'cabin boys', aka stewards, but it wasn't until the 1940s post war period that BOAC introduced their 'air hostess'! Needless to say, I preferred the term 'air steward' to 'cabin boy'!

But by the time I started BOAC still hadn't plucked up the courage to run combined training courses for the boys and girls!

2. FIRST FLIGHTS

'It Don't Come Easy'

Ringo Starr

*'In a short time, we will serve
refreshments. Please remember
that we are in the airline business,
not the food business.'*

A long with everyone else on the course, I started my career on Boeing 707s and Vickers VC-10s. The 707 carried one hundred and forty-six passengers. The VC10, depending on whether it was the Standard or Super version, up to one hundred and thirty-seven. For the aficionados, I flew on both 707 types - the ones with the Pratt and Whitney engines and those with Rolls Royce Conway engines. The combined fleet was affectionally known as the 'Elite Fleet' to those of us who flew on them. After the introduction of the 747, they then became 'The Mini Fleet'.

Boeing 707 foreground. Standard VC10 and two Super VC10's behind. (BA Speedbird Heritage Centre)

The Standard VC10 served BOAC's Middle East, Far East and African routes. Built specifically for BOAC, it was designed to accommodate the shorter runways found in those regions. The Super, with more passenger capacity, flew the high-density routes across the Atlantic. The tougher 707, less prone to mechanical gremlins and with a greater range, went everywhere and anywhere!

The starchy bureaucrats at the Board of Trade (now the Department for Transport) mandated we could only work on three planes at a time. For every type, we had to pass a written exam on safety procedures and equipment. The trick was remembering the differences on the aircraft when you were onboard. It was easy to confuse where the fire axe was on a VC10 Standard, compared to a Super or 707 – especially when you were asked the question by a training steward checking our knowledge on the job!

My favourite aircraft by far was the 707. Unkindly referred to as 'fifty thousand nuts and bolts flying in close formation', it had more galley space which make the job easier, despite its minor foible of having to wedge the fridge door closed with a coat hanger on take-off! Failure to do this resulted in the entire contents ending up on the galley floor as you gracefully, or otherwise, climbed towards the heavens! Due to its more flexible airframe, I also preferred the way the 707 flew. Its flexibility made the wings 'flap' up and down and the fuselage flex in turbulence, giving the plane the appearance of a huge metallic bird. Despite this, the 707 was a sturdy workhorse, one in which I always felt totally safe, whatever the weather.

By contrast, the VC10 had a more rigid airframe and had its engines at the tail, not under the wing. For passengers, the VC10 was a quieter plane to fly in making it a favourite with them. It was described as having 'hush power', which made me laugh. This was because it may have been quieter in the cabin but it was a noisy beast on the outside. The decibels generated by a fuel heavy VC10 on departure was off the scale. As a second steward, my take-off position was at the back, sitting next to the engines, so I had two Conway engines, at full throttle, in each ear! As the plane thundered down the runway, the noise from the engines was anything but hushed! Loud violence, more like! As we always had a steward and stewardess sitting together in the crew seats down the back this is where, despite the din, we would swap stories and gossip about others on the crew!

Both the 707 and VC10 had six cabin crew. A chief steward, a first and second steward, and three stewardesses. There were no female chiefs! The first steward and the 'A' lady worked in first-class. The second steward and the 'B' and 'C' birds, as they were called, looked after the economy cabin. The 'B' in 'B' birds stood for bogs, babies, and books! The role of the 'C' stewardess was often filled by our Chinese, Indian, Japanese, Singaporean, or Caribbean national girls. Hired for their language skills and cultural awareness, they worked the specific routes from their countries of origin. Dressed in national costume, the saris, cheongsams, or kimonos added an exotic element that suggested subservience and a sense of sexuality – the thigh slit in the cheongsam testament to that. Where national stewardesses weren't needed they were replaced by a 'C' bird based at Heathrow, our home base where all my trips started and ended. On arrival at the airport, we signed in at Crew Reporting in Building 221. This infamous office was in Terminal 3's South Office Block. Here we collected our bar float and white jackets, which could be as many as six depending on how long we were away for. Once we were all gathered, we took the crew transport out to the aircraft. Despite what ads might portray, in those days we didn't walk through the terminal. We only ever did this when we were down the routes! It was on the bus where we properly met up with the rest of our crew for the trip. As crews were never kept together, we always had a new crew every time. Some were great, some OK, and some not so OK! In the time it took to drive out to the plane, I knew which type of crew I belonged to and I quickly learned to recognise the type of crew it was! The chief steward set the tone – if he was a grumpy git the omens weren't good! The ride out to the plane gave a good indication of how much fun was to be had before getting back to Heathrow!

My first flight was across the 'Pond', aka the North Atlantic. This was as a supernumerary steward (an extra member of the crew) on a Washington bound Super VC10. Supernumerary trips were how new stewards and stewardesses transitioned from serving meals in the mock-up to the real deal. This trip, like the majority across the Atlantic, was three days. Arriving at the aircraft for my first flight was a huge milestone. The VC10's sleek design, with its blue and gold livery, was a magnificent sight. Whereas I was cloaked in nervous anticipation, the plane exhibited a confident elegance. Although I had flown before, I had never experienced a long-haul flight. I had never travelled further afield than Spain or Switzerland but now I was embarking on an adventure to another continent and I had, in every sense of the word, entered another world.

I loved flying and still do. The sensation, the thrill, and the power of it all is the best feeling. And to be a part of it as crew, was amazing. As I climbed the steps that first time my excitement was palpable and I will never forget the smell of kerosene jet fuel filling my nostrils – a smell I will forever associate with my days as an air steward. The scary bit was I was now the one in charge!

On entering the plane, I encountered another unmistakable smell. It's an aroma only aircraft of a certain vintage exude. The faint hint of a forgotten meal, a furtive scent of stale perfume, and a distinct whiff of air freshener.

My 'Speedbirds', sadly their names are lost over time!

The girls wore their blue and pink Clive summer uniform, and I thought they looked fantastic. However, not all the girls were keen on the dresses. Some thought the pink matched their eyes after a long night sector, others that they looked like nuns in mini-skirts! I was a fan, as were many male passengers! This could have been because of the way the dresses rode up when the girls were putting stuff into the overhead lockers! One thing the girls were all agreed on was that the elegant winter uniform was best, and definitely not as bad as the paper dresses they had had to wear a few years earlier on the Caribbean routes. Although fire-proof, the pop art-style paper dresses, emblazoned with purple flowers and green leaves, were not a hit. Perhaps this had something to do with the fact that they became see through if they got wet – so I am told! Mini-skirts weren't the sole domain of BOAC, quite the opposite. In the 1970s, the airline industry wasn't afraid to use the sex appeal of their stewardesses to put bums on seats. Southwest Airlines kitted their female crew out in thigh revealing ultra-short mini-skirts – much, much shorter than those worn by our girls. In 1971, National Airlines ran the infamous advert featuring a young stewardess with the slogan 'I'm Linda. Fly Me'. The implication was blatant enough! Our version of this trend, howwever, was a little more British in its approach!

BOAC 'Birds of Britain' press advertisement.
(BA Speedbird Heritage Centre)

The girls worked the cabin, and I looked after the rear galley and was responsible for the whole of the economy section. As this was my first trip, I was to work the sector under the guidance of the more experienced second steward. This was a great move. Others on my course went along and only got to observe how things were done; they didn't get the benefit of actually working the flight. The routine when we boarded, which I was now putting into practice for the first time, was to stow away your personal kit, check the safety and first aid equipment, check the galley equipment and make sure the power is on, and finally check that the bars were onboard and sealed!

We also had to ensure we actually had all the food and drink we needed for the flight. To leave without the correct number of meals was a cardinal sin! As I was working the flight, this meant I had to serve the meals hot and on time, as well as provide a continuous supply of alcohol, tea, and coffee. Measuring four foot by three and a half foot, the galley was somewhat bijou for the task, but it was well enough equipped with air larders, Mapco ovens, a fridge, a work surface, a hot-cup, and a sink. Everything I needed to dish out over one hundred plates of food - twice every flight!

Next, I set about making the coffee in a couple of the hot water boilers. It was important to fill them and get them on and heating up as early as possible. We used a brand of coffee called Mansion House, which, if memory serves, came in elegant gold foil packs. (The tea we dished up was called Windsor Castle.) As it took the boilers an age to heat up it could hardly be called instant coffee! I learnt later that when we were on a short sector, it also made sense to switch the oven on at the same time to give the meals the heating time they needed.

After we had settled the passengers onboard, I closed the rear door. Then it was back to the galley to check the equipment catches were secure for take-off. The last thing I needed was for one of these to come loose! As we taxied out, I double checked the catches again. Then, to feed my OCD traits, I checked a third time!

Whilst I was doing all this, we taxied out to the runway with the girls giving the life jacket demo. The girls normally did this job, and it was one I was happy to leave to them - they were far easier on the eye than I could ever be!

The plane was pretty near full in both first and economy - there being no such thing as business class in those days. The two cabins were separated with a curtain. On the other side of the curtain, life in first-class was properly 'posh'! Meat was not just served; it was carved in front of the passengers - using full size carving knives! Champagne, served in glass flutes, flowed from the moment passengers boarded. Cocktails and canapes were freely available. Lobster thermidor, served on Royal Doulton china, often on the menu. For their part, whatever side of the curtain they were on, passengers dressed up to fly. The days of dressing down in tracksuit bottoms were in the future. Appearances mattered; smart was the accepted order of the day. Men wore jacket and tie, women tailored twin set or posh frocks. First-class passengers were definitely a breed apart from their economy counterparts. With their declarative upper-class accents, they were an eclectic mix of privilege. The first-class passenger list was made up of oil executives, landed gentry, senior civil servants, actors, and minor royals from the Gulf and Brunei. And, as I was to discover later in my career, positioning crew!

One type of first-class traveller in particular fascinated me, and that was the Queen's Messenger. QMs were ex-service men, or retired high ranking civil servants, employed by the British Foreign and Commonwealth Office to travel the world delivering 'diplomatic papers' to our embassies and consulates. They usually had two seats to themselves; one for them and one for the briefcase that never left their side. It was a job I liked the look of, but my two-year stint as a Signalman in the Territorial Army (now the Army Reserve) would never qualify me for the position!

Even if the economy offering wasn't as grand, passengers were still very well looked after. Throughout the flight, passengers would get drinks, food, and then more drinks. True, we only gave them a plated meal on a plastic tray - not for them the silver service passengers got 'up front'. But we did have time to talk with them, unlike crews working today's battery hen economy cabins, making conversation commonplace and all part of the service!

As we powered down the runway and lifted gracefully into the air on this my first flight, I felt I had truly become an aviator!

When the captain switched off the 'No Smoking' signs the people sitting in the back rows lit up. Cigars and pipes were not allowed, but cigarettes were fine! Smoking bans didn't come into force until many years later. A lot of crew didn't like working at the back because of the smoke. I don't remember it being an issue, but as I was a smoker myself in those days, that may be why. As I was to discover, if there were any spare seats at the rear of the plane we would hang up a privacy curtain to create a rest area, a refuge from passengers where we could eat, sleep, or even have a quick fag ourselves! As strange as it may seem now, we actually sold cigarettes for passengers to smoke on the plane. Benson and Hedges, Players Navy Cut, and State Express being the brands of the time.

After the 'Fasten Seat Belts' sign went off, I sprang into action! I changed into my white jacket and headed to the galley. First order of the day was to check the power was still on and fire up the ovens and the hot cup. The hot cup was an evil little thing - spitting near boiling water at every opportunity but it did have its uses for heating babies' bottles and boiling eggs!

Then I had to organise the bar ready to dispense the drinks orders as the girls brought them in. For their part, the girls would set-up the first-class trolley and wheel it through the cabin offering free daily newspapers to passengers. After that, I had to convert it into a drinks trolley and go out, with one of the girls, to serve drinks while the meals were cooking.

We carried a range of spirits, cocktails, liqueurs, wine, and beers. Prices were in the recently introduced decimal currency. Beers were 15p a can, spirits and liqueurs 30p a miniature bottle, and champagne 65p a quarter bottle! The wine was French, such as a Fleurie. Fleurie is a well-known Cru Beaujolais which 'drank well' at thirty thousand feet. Although altitude doesn't affect the wine, it does affect our taste buds, they change inside a pressurised cabin making things taste different. As a result, wines that might be great to drink on the ground might not be so great in the air. And there are other properties wine has when drunk at altitude that can have unfortunate consequences. Due to pressurisation the human body can become dehydrated, and this has the effect of making every glass of wine, or any alcohol for that matter, three times more potent than it would have been down the local pub! Little wonder then that passengers often tottered down the steps a tad tipsy at the end of a long flight!

Against all my expectations, the lunch service went well. I put into practice everything I had been told in training and, much to my relief, there were no dramas, everyone got a meal perfectly heated, tea and coffee all drinkable. A natural, I think the chief steward said! He was obviously being encouraging; for my part I suspect my performance had been clumsy and halting - but his comments did my confidence no end of good!

Four hours later, although it seemed like the blink of an eye, I was at it again - this time serving afternoon tea or, as BOAC called it, 'Thé Anglaise'. Consisting of scotch salmon salad and apple tart, it might have had a fancy name but we still served the tea in a melamine cup!

Once again, the service went well and any doubts I may have privately harboured about my ability to handle the job disappeared.

Despite being my first trip, I still found the time to take in the view, which was wonderful! Cotton wool clouds and wispy strands of cirrus stretching across a bright blue sky. Takes some beating - all a far cry from the closed blinds in today's hi-tech cabins!

Before landing, I sealed the bar using a crimping tool and a metal tag ready for Customs to inspect on arrival. This was after counting the money and completing the paperwork – which involved filling in several forms. There was one for recording breakages and one to show the opening and closing stock balances, whilst another recorded what stock had been uplifted on the trip. There were also Custom declarations, bar discrepancies forms, and a form for the bar float, which showed all the cash transactions made. All in triplicate! I was quickly knee deep in red, green, and white copies!

As a Second Steward, I was responsible for the money and it was cash only, which created its own pressures. If I messed up the currency exhange, added up incorrectly, gave out the wrong change, or got the price wrong, passengers soon said something! A few passengers would falsely claim they had been short changed, but in most cases, a query was down to a genuine misunderstanding on their part about the exchange rate we used. Which absolutely wasn't to thier advantage! One trick I quickly devised was to write down my exchange calculations on a napkin in order to protect myself. This way, I had something to show how I had arrived at a number. If the passenger was trying to pull a move, they had to explain how their calculation differed! If I had made a genuine mistake, which I did from time to time, the reason for the error was there to explain it away! The exchange rate, by the way, was UK£1.00 to US$2.6057. I was always relieved at the end of a trip when my cash balanced with the number of drinks sold and the bottles left in the bar!

On arrival back at Heathrow the cash box and paperwork had to be handed in to a team of ladies, rubber thimbles on their fingers, who minutely checked the paperwork. There was no denying them. They could find even the smallest discrepancy. Fortunately, my paperwork was always in order, possibly down to my having worked in accountancy. Or maybe it had to do with something a little more 'imaginative'!

The trick was to avoid any shortfall in the first place. One of the best measures to ensure you always had the right money involved duty-free half bottles. Made of glass, they were prone to breaking on take-off if the bar wasn't full. The bottles could, and on occassion did, move around and smash, which were then written off as breakages. If the bar survived take-off and we didn't get breakages, we could still put down on the paperwork that we had some broken bottles! These 'broken bottles' were then sold and the proceeds went into the cash box to make up for any shortfall caused by my own limited maths ability! I know some stewards used this ploy to make a bit extra cash, pocketing the proceeds for themselves, but I never did. The job was worth more to me than that, plus it is not in my nature. I do confess to using it once or twice to make up the cash box, but nothing more than that. Of course, when plastic bottles replaced glass, stewards ended up with loads more cash discrepancies which they had to repay out of their own bank accounts! Ouch!

After eight and a half hours, tired but elated, we touched down in Washington and I had my first taste of 'slipping' down the routes. It was early evening and I had morphed into a real airline steward!

Despite feeling on a high as we drove in to the city from the airport, my first impression of Washington was one of real disappointment. I had expected to see skyscrapers everywhere, but there were none to be seen. Washington was all low rise, at least the parts we drove through were, and despite Washington having some of the most iconic landmarks in the world, I never got near them! I still haven't seen the White House, Lincoln Memorial, or Capitol Hill to this day.

In 1971, the year of this first trip, Washington was a dangerous city. Growing resentment against the Vietnam War fueled angry civil disobedience riots which happened regularly. The city also had a very high level of violence and robbery, making it, if I recollect correctly, the city with the second highest murder rate anywhere in the world. Because of this, crews were not allowed to leave the hotel. So, instead of going sightseeing I spent my first ever overseas rest day lounging around the pool in the company of bikini- clad hosties! I may not have got to see the local sights, but the view from where I sat was not too shabby!

After a day working on my soon-to-be permanent tan, it was back to work for the overnight flight to London. Immediately after departure, we served dinner and then 'bedded' passengers down for the night. Once again, it all went like clockwork and I diligently attended to my duties, such as they were, in the middle of the night. Apart from an odd drink, or the occasional call button, I had plenty of time to do my bar paperwork – which took up most of the flight! But I loved the atmosphere of the aircraft softly droning its way across the night sky as passengers slept after thier evening meal. There was a kind of hushed serenity about the cabin I really found captivating. By the time we taxied onto stand at Heathrow, having served breakfast and secured everything properly, I was knackered and, quite possibly, a little disheveled. I had survived. Now I was ready to go solo. What could possibly go wrong?

After the mandatory three nights off, I was back for my second flight – operating without the safety net of an experienced steward to watch over me! The trip was back across the pond, this time for the seven hour thirty-five-minute flight to New York.

When we got out to the aircraft, I was greeted by one of the catering loaders who came up to me and said, with a huge grin on his face, *"All seventy-six kosher meals are on."* My heart sank. One of the girls said *"Stop messing around, this is his first trip!"* Turned out he wasn't messing around; we did have seventy-six kosher meals on board and he knew how much of a problem they caused for stewards. My baptism of fire had well and truly begun because kosher meals had to conform to the religious dietary laws observant Jews adhere to. As our meals were certified by the Jewish rabbinical court Beth Din, this gave rise to us irreligiously referring to the meals as 'Bethlehem Dinners'! And the loader was right, the meals did represent a problem.

The first issue was the meals couldn't be heated in the same oven as non-kosher meals. But, sometimes load factors dictated they had to go in the same oven regardless, and when this happened we had to ensure no kosher meal was 'contaminated' by being dripped on by a gentile entré! The obvious solution was to stack the kosher meals above the others in the oven, which was fine until the trays had to be rotated half way through the heating time - which involved swopping the top and bottom trays around leaving the kosher meals at the bottom of the oven.

National stewardesses rotating meal trays. Food was cooked on the ground and then rapid chilled ready for us to heat. (BA Speedbird Heritage Centre)

As I had so many kosher meals on this flight, I was going to have to use the same oven for some of the meals. I had no choice. Anyway, as the meals were all sealed in foil, I figured a little gravy was not so bad and could be easily wiped off before going out to the passenger! Oy vey! The second issue was that we had to present the sealed tray to the passenger before heating it so they could see it conformed to Beth Din standards and the seal was still in place. Faced with doing this seventy-six times, I found the rabbi in charge of the group and got his approval instead! I may have been green, but I was learning quickly! But on my first trip I could have done without the hassle! The girls on the crew were great. They saw I was straight out of training and did all they could to help. Their support made a huge difference. So much so, everything went according to plan, despite the kosher complications!

After a text book flight where, despite all my nervousness about how I would cope on my own, we landed in New York early afternoon and everything had gone according to the book! The trip to the crew hotel took us into Manhattan, via the Queens Midtown Tunnel and, unlike Washington, New York totally lived up to my expectation. With skyscrapers everywhere, the Big Apple was exactly as I had seen it on the telly!

Our hotel was on Lexington Avenue, the hotel bearing the same name. Lexington Avenue was the setting for the classic 1955 movie, The Seven Year Itch, where the scene, in which Marilyn Monroe stands on a subway air vent with her skirt billowing up, was filmed.

With its grand entrance lobby and contrasting dark narrow corridors, the Lexington Hotel was the airline equivalent to a bee-hive. With crews coming and going at all hours, the place was in perpetual motion. And the hotel had its fair share of crew tales to tell. In one, a BOAC steward was beaten to the ground inside the lobby by New York's finest wielding night sticks. His 'crime'? He had run from the police when they had tried to stop him for some reason, which is rarely a good idea especially in New York. Predictably, the cops took chase assuming he was guilty of something and, when they caught up with him, beat him to a pulp - well, almost. It turned out he had done nothing wrong – and an apology came there none! In another story, a steward or pilot, I'm not sure which, took up a ridiculous bet. To win, he had to swing outside his bedroom window, ten stories up, using the curtains as a rope! Guess what? You can't cure stupid!

Bed bugs often featured in tales about the place. Because the hotel had such a constant turnover of crew, a lot of people reported being bitten by the little critters, which didn't surprise me. Such was the turnover of crew through the hotel that on one trip I got into bed to find the mattress still warm from the previous occupant. Fortunately, I never got bitten. Too sour, probably.

Whatever you felt about the hotel, it was a great location for exploring central Manhattan. Unlike some crew members, who preferred to stay in the hotel or a bar close by, I wanted to experience the city. And after the curfew of Washington, I was raring to go!

I had the late afternoon and evening the day I arrived, and most of the next day to myself. Ample time to get around the city. My preferred method of travel was by yellow cab, although others used the subway or shank's pony. Over the years, I went up The Empire State Building, around Central Park, into Macey's, across Times Square, down Broadway, along 5th Avenue, and climbed the Statue of Liberty - from the inside that is! I especially remember the Statue of Liberty – and not for the reason you might imagine! The statue has a viewing platform in the crown that was open to the public and, despite my fear of heights, I decided to go up. To reach the viewing platform I had to climb a tight circular staircase and I just happened to be following two Hawaiian girls who both had the most amazing pair of bronzed legs – set off by the shortest of short miniskirts. It gave a whole new meaning to the term 'seeing the sights'! Oh yes, the view from the twenty-five windows in the crown looking out across New York Harbour wasn't too bad either! Funny the things that stick in your mind!

One of the places crew headed for in New York was the Bowery, otherwise known as 'Skid Row'. This was where the homeless 'Bowery Bums' congregated and it was not an edifying sight. Homeless down-and-outs, with booze bottle in hand, living in squalor on the streets, slumped in doorways shouting obscenities at passers-by hardly qualified the area as a tourist attraction. Yet, bizarre as it sounds, it was of sorts. Nowadays, we'd call it slum or ghetto tourism. For someone like me, living in picturesque Kent, it was a shocking experience that I will never forget. As odd as it sounds, we were helping to shape and create that form of tourism, which is now commonplace in the favelas of Rio or the slums of Mumbai.

New York was always a profitable trip. This was because the daily allowances we received were generous. Which was more than it was in a lot of places. Paid on arrival in dollars, the allowance was intended to cover our hotel food costs for the layover. Rather than spend it at the hotel, we would find the cheapest local diner we could! Some crew even went as far as taking food off the plane to supplement their rations! The food was 'harvested' from unused meal trays, yielding bread rolls, soft cheese triangles, peanuts, and teabags - amongst other things. I never bothered. Instead, I headed to TADS Steak House to get a cheap meal. And TADS was cheap – in every sense of the word! I could get a steak there for a dollar ninety-nine! With its strong smell of meat smoke, there was no mistaking the place for a classy joint! That aside, I managed to eat and pocket most of my meal allowance into the bargain! Many years later I took my wife to a TADS in Times Square – the last one standing. To say she was not impressed is a massive understatement!

On this first trip to New York, I rose early the

next day and had one of those fabulous American breakfasts. I spent the morning ambling around the streets, soaking up the atmosphere. A lot of crew, especially the girls, treated New York purely as a shopping trip. To be fair, goods were very cheap compared to back home and, in some cases, the stuff wasn't yet available in the UK, but I loved just ambling about the place soaking up the atmosphere. After returning to the hotel around midday, I grabbed an afternoon siesta. Then it was off to the coffee shop for hash browns and eggs, before boarding the crew bus for the return trip to JFK. Little did I know it, but this was to be my regular routine for every New York night stop I ever did! If it ain't broke, don't fix it!

The return flight to London was a carbon copy of the trip on the way out. Everything ran smoothly, so I remember little about that flight, except for the Northern Lights. It was my first, and only, sighting of them. Albeit a fleeting one.

Economy-class meal service. (BA Speedbird Heritage Centre)

We were serving dinner when the captain announced that the lights could be seen on the port side of the plane. I took a quick peek. I got a glimpse of a greenish colour in the night sky before returning my attention to the galley. It was so fleeting a glimpse that I really don't feel I can truly claim to have seen them.

As we landed back at Heathrow, I felt proud of myself. I had earned my wing, survived my first transatlantic crossing, and realised two things.

One, the job was hard work.

Two, the glamour was about where we went and not so much about what happened in the air!

3. ACROSS THE POND

'Get It On'

T Rex

*'We are now going to attempt
to fly to New York.'*

I found myself rostered across the Atlantic a lot; we all did. A major feature of these trips was the weather, so turbulence was a constant companion thanks to the jet stream. The jet stream is a band of wind that blows from west to east across the Atlantic, making for a bumpy ride on many flights. Flying out to the States, the plane has to battle headwinds all the way whereas, coming back, the plane is merrily pushed along by a strong tailwind, making the return trip about an hour faster. Either way, it did make the aircraft move a bit!

Turbulence happens. It's like waves on the sea, some waves bigger than others. So too with turbulence. Few passengers like it and some are genuinely scared when it happens. They think the turbulence will cause the plane to crash but it won't, planes can tolerate normal and severe levels of turbulence very well.

Normal turbulence is the sort most people experience. It's not dangerous and is commonplace. This sort of turbulence makes tea tremble in its cup, nothing more.

Severe turbulence causes a plane to jump around and makes the wings move up and down and planes are designed to take this sort of treatment, easily coping with the stresses and strains placed on them. It may feel alarming to passengers, but the plane is not in any danger.

So far so good, but extreme turbulence can cause a plane to be tossed around the skies. In extreme conditions, this can cause structural damage that may imperil the plane and its passengers. In this type of turbulence, objects would be flying around the cabin and overhead lockers breaking open and disgorging thier contents on the heads of passengers. But extreme turbulence is very rare ,and is normally associated with thunderstorms which can be dangerous if the pilot flies into or close to the thunder clouds. Because of this, commercial airline pilots always avoid thunder clouds. Modern weather radars give pilots ample information enabling them to fly round thunderstorms and avoid them completely. Consequently, thunderstorms and, by association, extreme turbulence, isn't something passengers need to worry about.

Cabin crew are more vulnerable to injury during turbulence than passengers because they are moving around the cabin, and over the years some have been badly injured by unexpected turbulence. Nowadays, there is a much greater awareness of the danger to crews and I see them sitting down far more now in realitively light turbulence than we ever did. We only strapped in when the going got really rough!

One misconception about turbulence is that it causes airsickness. It can, but it isn't always the case! Airsickness strikes when the eyes tell the brain that things around them are not moving although the inner ear is telling the brain the body is moving. For example, someone sitting reading a book is focused on an object that's not moving – the book. The relationship between the book and the eyes is not changing or moving. But the plane is and your inner ear knows it, the conflict between the two results in vomit! And it can be 'contagious'. I found this out on one flight where we had a contingent of Japanese passengers onboard. Flying conditions were good, but there was a very gentle 'chop' causing the plane to move around a little but not enough to induce airsickness. Or so I thought!

It began when one woman started chucking up and this 'encouraged' the person next to her to join in. And then the person next to her got in on the act. Soon enough, the domino effect kicked in and within minutes the whole group were honking away like geese in a farmyard. In no time at all, the cabin reeked with the stink of puke. The normal quiet of the cabin was resounding to the sound of retching! Not being good around people being sick, I would normally have joined in but on this occasion I stepped up and acted as the professional I had become! Amid all this, there I am, with a stewardess, mincing up and down the aisle dishing out cold towels and cuspidors to every beseeching hand that reached out for one! As the ads said 'BOAC takes good care of you', but I wasn't sure where this was in the job description! It felt like we were going above and beyond for sure. The worst bit was collecting the now full cuspidors back in to dispose of them. Still warm, not fun! It's that glamour thing again! At least, it was better than having to fish a passenger's false teeth out of the loo, which did happen on occassion. I have no idea what caused the teeth to end up there in the first place, but after a quick rinse the grateful passenger just popped the teeth back in! Yuk!

Turbulence wasn't the only weather issue we encountered. Fog was a massive problem, especially at Heathrow. Heathrow was often closed in the early morning during winter months so this meant arriving flights had to be diverted to Manchester; known in the trade as a 'div day'.

On one such trip, we pitched up at Manchester and as our VC10 taxied to a stop, the apron around us was full to capacity with every imaginable airline, all having arrived there because of the fog. We were in good company, including a couple of other BOAC planes parked nearby. Unseen by us, the terminal was heaving with passengers, many of whom were earlier arrivals waiting to re-board as soon as the fog at Heathrow lifted. Consequently, we couldn't get our folk off the plane.

As we couldn't disembark passengers, they had to stay on the plane. But as one hour became two, then three, then four, tempers frayed. All attempts by the captain to get our passengers off came to naught. We did what we could to make them as comfortable as possible, but it was difficult. We only had tea and coffee to offer them as the bars had to remain sealed because of Custom's regulations, and we had served all the food during the flight. Because of the number of planes on the ground, any attempt to try and get additional catering loaded was out of the question. After six hours the joke had worn a bit thin. Actually, things were a bit grim by that stage. It was becoming an increasing struggle to keep the loos in a reasonable condition, and any passenger goodwill that might have been present when we landed had long since evaporated. Passengers were becoming increasingly angry, unsurprisingly, at being held captive on the plane. Not that I had a great deal of sympathy with them at the time. They were sitting down. They could have a snooze. They could read a book. It wasn't the crew holding them on the plane, it was the airport's refusal to let them off that was the issue. And we were still on duty, walking up and down six hours after finishing a six-hour Atlantic night flight!

Mercifully, after seven hours our flight engineer ran out of hours so this meant the whole crew couldn't work anymore that day. So, even if the fog lifted at Heathrow, we couldn't have flown them there that day. It would have required a new crew being brought up from London to take the flight. Given this new situation, the airport finally had no option but to offload our passengers and make arrangements for them to complete their journey by train. We managed to get off the plane and headed, dog tired, to the Manchester Grand for a well-earned rest. The next morning, on a bright and fog free day, we flew our empty plane down to London.

It was a different experience – without passengers the job was a doddle!

By all accounts, things on one of our 747's had been a great deal worse. In a similar situation to ourselves, they also couldn't offload their passengers. Things had reached breaking point when an argument between two passengers escalated into a no-holes barred fist fight. During the ensuing fracas, one of the stewards intervened to stop the fight and ended up being punched for his efforts, resulting in him requiring medical attention! Don't remember that on the training course!

Heathrow wasn't the only place where weather could be a problem. New York, for example, could be a challenging place to fly into in winter. This was especially true of one flight I was on heading for New York's JFK airport from Montego Bay.

We had left the Caribbean with temperatures in the high twenties, while New York was in the grip of wintery sub-zero temperatures. This was to become the second drama of the trip, the first caused mainly by a farcical series of events during an aborted landing on our arrival at Montego Bay.

As we made our approach into Montego Bay, with a first officer fresh out of training school at the controls, it was obvious the approach was too high. From my rear seat, I saw the touch down zone markings on the runway pass below us meaning it would have to be a hell of a flare, when the power is reduced to allow the aircraft to touch down smoothly (performed at around fifteen feet off the runway), if we were to land in time! We were well above fifteen feet and any flare would probably have resulted in us breaking the aircraft's back as we made contact with the ground. Gamely, the 'junior jet', our name for newbie first officers, continued to try and land but we inevitably ran out of runway without having come close to the asphalt surface! We duly abandoned the approach when the captain took over control, applying full power to the engines that propelled us skywards. Normally, a go-around, as this is called, was no big deal but this one was to prove different. The root of the problem was that the chief steward had left starting the meal service before our arrival too long, leaving us with not enough time to get all the trays back in and stowed before landing.

As luck would have it, we had a training steward on the flight which gave us an extra pair of hands. Training stewards carried out periodic checks on the crew, the main purpose being to see if we knew where the safety equipment was located on the air-craft and how we performed on the job in general. With time running out, Len, our training steward this day, had come up with the bright idea of stack-ing trays on the galley worktop - where he would stand and hold them steady for landing. Once on the ground, we could stow them away at leisure. Of course, the plan assumed a normal landing, where the stacked trays would fall against the front wall of the galley and be easily kept in place by our erstwhile colleague.

As Sod's Law dictates, this went horrible awry when we began the go-around and the forces of nature came into play, resulting in the inevitable! The trays, no longer wanting to lean toward the front of the plane, went in the opposite direction landing on the floor in a spectacular display of mayhem! Totally unprepared for this sudden change in speed and direction Len also went tumbling back and down, ending up on the galley floor covered head to toe in the detritus of some one-hundred used meal trays! From my seat next to the galley, I had a ringside view. It was carnage! It was, also, side-splittingly funny! The state of both the galley floor, and Len, was something to behold. With a myriad of half-eaten bits of food all over him, he made my white jacket look clean!

The punchline to this story is that Len was something of a BOAC celebrity. As a young steward in 1952, he was on a BOAC Hermes bound for Kano in Nigeria when it got lost over the desert because the navigator made an error that went unnoticed by the rest of the crew, until it was too late. When they realised they were totally off course they no longer had sufficient fuel to make it to any airfield.

The plane crash landed in the deserts of Mauritania when the fuel ran out, forcing the pilot to make a wheels-up landing. Amazingly, the only serious injury to anyone on board was sustained by the First Officer. The group were found by Bedouin nomads who set up a camp using their own tents. A search plane located them and dropped emergency supplies, radioing the crash site co-ordinates to a rescue party being assembled. It was at this point the fortunes of the survivors started to wane. The rescue party failed to reach them, defeated by the extreme conditions. With the First Officer's condition worsening, the group took the decision to strike camp and venture out in search of medical attention for him. Travelling on camels at night to avoid the heat of the day, after only sixteen hours they were forced to stop – unable to continue because of severe sandstorms. Sadly, the First Officer died before the group were able to move off again.

With the group in increasing peril, Len volunteered to go off on his own in search of help. Despite all the odds, he managed to find help and led them back to the group. For his actions, he received a commendation for bravery. To end up on a galley floor, covered in garbage, just didn't seem fitting!

With that all fading into memory the first sign of a second drama, and a serious one at that, came when the flight deck told us of the worsening weather at JFK. As we headed up the east coast, it became clear the weather was deteriorating fast, right across the eastern seaboard. We listened to air traffic control as airport after airport closed, including our own divert airport. With the divert shut, if New York also closed we were in something of a pickle because we didn't have the fuel to reach any of the other places still open and we didn't have the benefit of a nice sandy desert to put down in! Fortunately for us, JFK defied the weather and stayed open. As we started our final approach, there were three other planes ahead of us and another BOAC aircraft immediately behind. In front, there was Pan Am, TWA, and United who all tried to land, and who all abandoned the attempt. All three went round for another try. As we descended, the cabin was quiet with a sense of apprehension as it was obvious to one and all the weather outside wasn't exactly clement. Armed with a flashlight, I was ready for anything. The fact I was carrying a flashlight meant things might not turn out as well as we hoped! I strapped in for an uncertain landing.

After an extremely lumpy approach, buffeted by strong winds that bounced us around a lot, we made the landing. In the end, it was all very routine. And clearly, the 'junior jet' who had been at the controls on arrival in Jamaica, hadn't been entrusted with the landing this time round! The BOAC plane behind us followed us down and also landed without incident. Pan Am, TWA, and

United all opted not to try again and headed for thier respective diverts. Of all the planes that tried to land that night, we were the only two that made it; all the others chickened out and went elsewhere. Well, at least they had that option that night whereas New York was Hobson's Choice for us! Strike one for the skill of our pilots for having nailed the landing in such dreadful conditions!

It wasn't until we got off the plane that the enormity of the storm became clear. Snow was driving across the apron, stinging our faces as it came at us almost horizontal. The apron lights were barely visible. Snow ploughs could be seen battling mounting snow drifts and it was freezing. Coming from the warmth of the cabin and wearing only our normal uniforms, the cold went through to the bone in an instant.

Despite their lack of airmanship that night, I was always a little in awe of Pan Am, who were definately BOAC biggest rival.

We served eighty-cities in fifty-three countries across six continents; Pan Am flew to more places. Our home base was Hounslow; they had the Big Apple! We had a fleet of two hundred planes, they had more! We were well paid - you get the picture! For all these reasons I came to the conclusion that I wanted to work for them and live in New York. After flying with BOAC for a few months, I applied

- only to discover they weren't hiring at that time. Although I was invited to re-apply in the future, I never did get around to it!

****

New York was a high-volume route with hundreds of air passengers travelling to and from there daily. It was also a hub for BOAC, serving other routes such as some Caribbean islands and Bermuda. If my roster included the infamous Bermuda Shuttle out of New York, I worked London to New York and then, after a night stop, flew a return trip to Bermuda going out in the morning and back in the afternoon. After another night-stop in the Big Apple, it was back to London the following evening on the red-eye.

Referred to by some as the Daily Miracle, the Bermuda Shuttle was one of the toughest trips we did. We had to serve drinks and a full meal on each sector, both of which were around two hours flying time. We had to work fast, often only getting the meal trays in as we touched down! And there was never a training steward around to give us a helping hand! Some days crew did get off the plane in Bermuda to grab a milk shake in the terminal but I never did, I was always far too busy prepping for the return flight!

Bermuda Airport. (BA Speedbird Heritage Centre)

Aside from the Bermuda trip, we only did one other 'there-and-back-in-a-day' malarkey. And that was a Saturday holiday charter flight out of London to Munich on behalf of Erna Low, a specialist travel company. I worked it once, and it was the only time I ever turned up at Crew Reporting having left my passport at home! Fortunately, the chief steward decided I could still go as we wouldn't disembark in Munich. I'm not sure what would have happened if we'd gone tech on the ground there. I would have had to bed down on the plane!

Whilst both were holiday flights, the contrast between the two couldn't have been greater. On the Bermuda Shuttle, halter necks and short shorts were de-rigueur. Whereas on the Erna Low flight, bobble-hatted passengers carried their own body weight in kit and caboodle! And the contrast between the outbound and return leg on the Munich trip was just as striking. On the way out to Munich we carried a bunch of happy trippers heading for the ski slopes, and on the way back we brought home a bunch of medical cases! There were people on crutches, some with arms in slings, even one on a stretcher. The scene resembled a mercy flight! The sight of this motley band coming across the apron put me off skiing for the rest of my life!

It made the Daily Miracle feel like a walk in the park!

****

Over the years, the transatlantic routes had seen their fair share of disasters and dramas. Although the Atlantic was no more dangerous than flying anywhere else, with only the ocean below our feet for three and a half thousand miles it felt like it was. Perhaps it also had something to do with what happened in the pool with the life raft? More probably, any sense of this I may have had came, from an incident that took place one day in June 1972. I was in my seat at the back of the plane as we waited on the runway at Heathrow for our take-off clearance. But this was the day after the Trident Staines air disaster, the deadliest crash in the UK at that time, so twenty-four hours earlier to the minute, a BEA flight to Brussels had departed from the same runway. Three minutes later it crashed near Staines, killing everyone on board. It was an eerie sensation to be in exactly the same spot that those BEA passengers and crew had been in just the day before. Looking down our plane, with everythiing routine and normal, it was difficult to imagine everyone on board dying in less than four minutes time. It sent a chill down my spine. It still does.

But accidents were part and parcel of flying in the 1970s. It is difficult to believe how many aircraft were lost around this time, compared to how safe flying has become today. During the time I flew with BOAC there were forty-two fatal accidents, taking the lives of more than three thousand people. Obviously, this was not just BOAC, but the total for all airlines. To underline this peril, on the day I finished my training course, 31 July 1971, there were two crashes. One involved an All-Nippon Airways Boeing 727, the other a Pan Am Boeing 747. These two crashes alone claimed a total of one hundred and sixty-two lives. As crew, we regarded accidents as a numbers game because they tended to happen in pairs. When there had been two crashes, we felt we could relax - safe for a time! Analysis of the interval between accidents shows they often did occur within days of one another. So, there was a certain logic to the superstition!

And the state of our engines didn't help, with engine breakdowns a constant thorn in our side. It was not unheard of for the VC10's Rolls Royce Conway engines to explode, which, inconveniently, occasionally happened on take-off! Happily, I never experienced such excitement, but some crews did. When it happened, it was only the professionalism of the pilots that, quite literally, saved the day.

Flight engineer and ground staff fixing the engine
on a VC10 before our departure!

Accidents and exploding engines aside, we also had to contend with jet lag. Criss-crossing time zones and getting up when you should be going to bed took its toll on everyone. Transatlantic trips, for me, were the worst. There was one roster that had me dead on my feet. It involved crossing the Atlantic on an almost daily basis across a five-day period. These trips were London - New York -

Birmingham – New York – London, or London - Toronto - Manchester - Toronto - London. Four transatlantic crossings in five days! On each crossing, the girls would walk about seven miles, and I did a fair few just around the galley. By the time I got back to Heathrow at the end of one of these little marvels I was definitely a tad discombobulated!

Saviour came in the form of a pill! When my mojo flagged, which it did frequently, and no one wants a frequently flagging mojo, I would pop a couple of 'No Doz' tablets which I bought in New York. You couldn't get them in Britain at the time due to their obscene caffeine levels. Along with a quick pick-me-up landing drink they worked miracles, but when they wore off I went into total meltdown. I lost count of the times I had to pull into a lay-by for a sleep on the drive home from the airport because the tablet had worn off.

At nine hours and twenty minutes, the longest Atlantic crossing was to Miami. One of America's party-by-the-sea cities came complete with palm trees, casino hotels, and wide beaches. But it had seen better days. Gone were the days of Sinatra and Presley topping the bill at the Fontainebleau, although the Fontainebleau still had a lot going for it. But Ocean Drive and the Beach, nowadays the place where the rich and famous once again hang out, was lined with frayed hotels. Our crew hotel was one of them, populated only by the old and us lot. Not a youthful bronzed body in sight!

Miami, in keeping with its general decline and because it had the largest immigrant population in the States, and therefore a poor population, had some challenging areas downtown away from the beach. The Havana replica that is Miami today, with the pristine Art Deco renaissance buildings, was ten years in the future – waiting for Crocket and Tubbs in Miami Vice with its pink painted houses to kick start a revival.

So, I forsook the beach, downtown, and Ocean Drive, and headed for the Everglades - the world's most famous swamp. I loved riding the fan boats, or air boats as they are also called. They are small flat bottom craft with a huge propeller mounted on the back. Achieving speeds up to forty miles an hour, they are exhilarating to ride. The water isn't deep, about five feet in most places, making it the perfect alligator habitat. Every time I visited Miami I drove out through Cooperstown and jumped on a fan boat to commune with the 'gators!

Miami was where I experienced my first ever tropical storm. I had never seen wind and rain like it. When the storm hit, I was in my hotel room and glad I wasn't out on the streets, or on a boat in the Everglades! Within seconds, I couldn't see across the road. It was like standing behind a waterfall with a solid curtain of water in front of me. When the rain stopped, the city appeared to be boiling with steam coming off every surface as the sun re-asserted itself and the rain evaporated. I was to see many tropical storms as a steward, but that first one left an indelible memory.

For some reason, I particularly remember three things that happened to me on the Miami run.

The first was on a return flight to London; it was a little before departure and we were taxiing out to the runway. I had checked all the stowage catches were on, as usual, so was pretty confident nothing in the galley would shift on take-off. I was in my seat with my harness on, chatting with the stewardess next to me, when it hit me. I hadn't wedged a coat hanger into the front of the fridge door! This being a 707, it was always prudent to do that and here's why. As soon as we took off, the fridge doors swung open and the entire contents of the fridge looked like a stick of paratroopers about to jump and head for the galley floor. Strapped in to my full harness, I could only watch as the drama unfolded, unable to do very much about it. I knew it would only be a matter of seconds before the galley was awash with milk and other goodies. But, amazingly and inexplixably, nothing happened. The contents stayed put. How was this possible? No idea! Talk about a daily miracle! I have no idea how I got away with it, but it was the last time I ever forgot to wedge the door shut!

The second thing I remember involved discovering how we dealt with passenger complaints. Any passenger moved to make a complaint about the service was encouraged to fill in a customer complaint form. This form went straight to the chief steward who would include it in his flight report so management back at Heathrow could take the appropriate action. Only that never happened. To the best of my knowledge, all complaint forms were dealt with on board. Well, they went straight in the bin! This was how we achieved such high passenger satisfaction ratings! If passengers wanted their complaint to be heard, they had to be a bit more creative and take a leaf out of The Beatles book of complaining! In their song, 'Back in the USSR', the Beetles wrote the immortal lyrics:

'Flew in from Miami Beach BOAC,

Didn't get to bed last night,

On the way the paper bag was on my knee,

Man, I had a dreadful flight......'

That said, and despite the treatment of forms, we were pretty good at our job and took the whole matter of passenger satisfaction seriously. Most of the people I have ever meet who flew with the airline have very fond, and very complimentary memories, about their onboard experience.

The third thing related to the in-flight movies. We did have them, of sorts! Because of the flight time to Miami, 707's were used on the route and, unlike the VC10, they were equipped with film projectors! Of course, there were no screens in the seat backs as is the case nowadays. Instead, we had a projector mounted on the ceiling and screens that we pulled down from the roof. As they came down in the centre of the aisle it made moving about the cabin less than ideal. To reach a passenger who had rung their call bell, we had to limbo under the screens to reach them! Two screens in economy-class made life twice as difficult! Whoever invented them had never worked as cabin crew! And guess what? The projectors weren't that reliable so it wasn't unknown for them to break down mid film!

On one Miami flight, a projector stopped working when the drive belt snapped. At this point, help from the flight deck was apparently sought, and the Senior First Officer obliged. He replaced the belt with a makeshift one using a pair of tights donated by one of the stewardesses. A spare pair, hopefully! In the end, it took two pairs of tights to get the projector working again. I'm told the passengers didn't think much of the film, but did enjoy the cabaret act! A more common problem was when the film worked loose on the reel. Yes, it was a spool of old-style film that often entangled itself inside the projector. When this happened, it came out looking like spaghetti, for which no amount of nylon could fix.

Talking of stewardesses' tights, it brings to mind a prank played by the first-class steward that involved the said item with the flight crew as the target. When the plane was on final approach, and the crew focused on making a safe landing, the steward would open the flight deck door and throw in a pair of tights whilst announcing "'*A' bird's tights are off*!" Aimed right, and with enough heft, they would land slap bang in the middle of the instrument panel between the pilots. Given this is a critical time on the flight deck, I'm amazed pilots weren't distracted by these juvenile antics! And it wasn't only tights that went sailing through the air. On occasion, a pair of knickers was substituted for the tights! Once again, I have no idea where those came from!

****

On transatlantic flights we always left passengers to sleep as long as possible before waking them up for breakfast. It was the chief steward's decision when breakfast was served which, if left too late, was a recipe for chaos! Somewhere over the Bristol Channel, about twenty minutes out from

Heathrow, we started our descent. At this point, we would be busy stowing away the breakfast trays, collecting money from passengers for their drinks, doing the paperwork, and securing the galley in preparation for landing. This activity wasn't helped by the early morning toilet queue that snaked past the galley and made getting in and out of it all the more difficult!With all this going on, it wasn't uncommon to get a call from the front galley telling us we had made up time and we were landing ten minutes early! At this point, I would be on my hands and knees shoving used trays into their storage containers to make up time, my normally pristine white jacket covered in bits of half-eaten croissants, marmalade drips, and green omelette! This was the glamour I had signed up for!

If things got really tight and we couldn't stow the trays away in time, we had to employ some desperate measures. We couldn't just leave them with the passengers, as this would have been a serious safety risk. We had to get them away, whatever happened. If we did run out of time and couldn't get them properly stowed we opened the toilet door and chucked the used trays in, closing the door on them. Problem solved! Even though the breakfast tray was only a half tray, with cup and saucer, fruit bowl, plate, salt and pepper pots, and cutlery, the result was a spectacular mess! To the poor devils who had to come onboard and clean the aircraft at the end of the flight, it was an act of pure vandalism! But that didn't stop us from doing it as we were the ones at the sharp end and we were in the business of finding solutions to any problem we encountered in the air! Needs must and all that, your Honour! This only ever happened landing back into Heathrow; we couldn't do it down the routes as there wasn't enough time to clean it up on a forty-five minute turnaround!

At the end of a long eastbound transatlantic night flight crew sometimes enjoyed a 'landing drink'.

Once the cabin was sorted out for landing, the chief steward would walk down the plane carrying a teapot to the rear galley. To all intents and purposes, it was just a teapot. But it wasn't. It contained a small amount of champagne!

Of course, there were very strict rules on drinking alcohol onboard, for obvious reasons, and it was completely prohibited. Yet that didn't stop it from happening. It was a bit of a tradition and the only instance where crew ignored the no-alcohol rule. To be fair, the amount of champagne we consumed would do very little to endanger the plane, and there was a definite benefit for the passengers. A small snifter of champagne helped put a smile on our face as we bade them farewell!

4. RITES OF PASSAGE

'Send In The Clowns'

Judy Collins

'All the world's a stage.'

P ranks by aircrew were nothing new. As far back as the 1950s, crew were at it. Take, for example, one legendary BEA captain. One of his pranks involved climbing the aircraft stairs, in full view of the passengers, wearing dark glasses and tapping his way up the stairs with a white cane. Whatever else passengers might want from a crew, a blind pilot ain't one of them!

Another of his pranks involved a ball of string. In the Viscount, one of the planes flown by BEA, the toilet was situated behind the first rows of seats on the right-hand side. If the pilots wanted to use the toilet, they had to pass passengers to reach it. In this stunt, the captain emerges from the flight deck carrying two pieces of string. He stops at one of the passengers in the first row and asks them to hold the string - one in each hand. He tells them he is going to the toilet and, because of this, the co-pilot is a bit busy being left on his own on the flight deck. Could the passenger help? Would they mind holding the string for him? Just until he returns from the loo. Handing them the two bits of string, he explains how they can help. To assist the co-pilot they just need to keep the wings nice and level. But if the plane should start to turn towards the right, they must pull on the left-hand string to correct the movement. And vice versa if the plane went the other way. After explaining they will know when the plane is turning because the wing on that side will go down, he enters the toilet. On the flight deck, the co-pilot sets about putting the plane into a series of increasingly steep left and right turns, leaving the hapless passenger pulling on the strings to level the wings! Were passengers that gullible in those days? Were passengers ever let in on the joke? I have no idea on both counts. It all reminds me of the Monty Phyton airplane sketch, which ended up with all the passengers jumping out!

When it came to pranks, I was more than happy to

continue the noble art started back in the Viscount days. My favourite, played on newbie steward-esses, involved a life jacket. During the course of the demo, the stewardess would produce a whistle when they got to the part of the briefing that goes: 'there is a whistle here for attracting attention'. At this point, the stewardess holds the whistle up for all to see. What I, and other stewards did, was switch the whistle for a tampon we took from the passenger's vanity box. So, instead of holding a whistle the poor unfortunate girl is proudly dis-playing a tampon – much to my amusement. The girl's face was an absolute picture, and her blushes obvious. Boys will be boys!

Another wheeze, again aimed at newbie girls, in-volved substituting the inert dummy life jacket used in the briefing with a live one. At the point when it says, 'to inflate, pull the red toggle as shown' the stewardess gives the toggle a firm tug. As she does so, the life jacket bursts into life and fully inflates! Apart from the total surprise on her face, she now has to cope with completing the safety briefing wearing an impossibly bulky life jacket. It may well have scared the bejesus out of them, but it never failed to brighten my day!

I also heard of, but never saw, another prank played on new recruits. Shortly before starting the descent, the flight engineer comes down the cabin and tells the stewardess there is a technical problem with the undercarriage - it won't go down and he needs her help to fix it! He asks if she wouldn't mind jumping up and down in the middle of the plane to free the undercarriage just so they can land! I can picture the scene, but I'm not sure how many would have fallen for it!

And then there was the melting hat trick – pure genius. And yes, I definately played this one!

The girls didn't wear their hats during a flight so, if we were flying to somewhere hot like the Gulf or India, I offered to keep their hat cool for them for when we arrived. Once I had my hands on the hat I'd stick in the fridge ice box. After landing, I'd give the hat back just as they set off to say goodbye to our passengers, having knocked off any tell-tale frosting from the outside! Standing by the door, with outside temperatures in the forties, when the door opens a blast of hot air rushes into the cabin and the ice I had considerately left on the inside melts instantly! So, there she is, saying goodbye to passengers, smile in place while her carefully applied Elizabeth Arden mascara trickles down her face, making her look for all the world as if she had just got out of a swimming pool. Passengers loved it; they always saw the funny side but I'm not sure the poor girls did!

Another prank was the 'galley on fire' routine. This involved dry ice which we used down the routes to keep food containers cool. If the ice was put into the sink it melted, giving off clouds of white 'smoke' in the process. As this was heavier than air, it spilled over the worktop and fell to the floor where it accumulated. Left long enough, and with the galley curtain closed, a cloud of the stuff built up on the floor. Eventually, the 'smoke' would find its way out into the cabin from under the curtain. From a distance, it looked like the galley was on fire! When you pointed this out to a rookie stewardess the look on their face on seeing the 'smoke' was priceless! I would then play the big hero and enter the galley. After clattering a few pots about I'd re-emerge saying it was now sorted! It worked every time! Not sure the passengers sitting in the last rows at the back appreciated it and, to be fair, fire on a plane ain't a good thing!

But it wasn't just us lot down the back who played games, the flight deck also joined in. They had a couple of wizard pranks, both of them on the VC10.

The first was the 'voice operated throttle', played on both new crew and passengers alike. The VC10 had two sets of throttle levers. One set was located in the panel between the pilots, the other low down near the flight engineer's panel. This set allowed the flight engineer to operate the throttle, which he could do without being seen by the unsuspecting victim. The captain would explain how technically advanced the plane was, so much so it had voice operated controls. Today, speaking to appliances may not seem a big deal, but in the early 1970s it hadn't been invented - unless of course you were flying on a VC10!

The captain would demonstrate how it worked. He would instruct the plane to reduce engine power, and the throttle levers between him and the co-pilot would move accordingly. He would then repeat the process asking for more power. Again, the levers moved. Then the captain would offer visitors the opportunity to try it for themselves. Of course, when the visitor first spoke nothing happened; they had to speak louder and then the throttles responded. The passengers could make the plane speed up, or slow down! They were suitably impressed and left the flight deck to relay the story to their travelling companions. Worked a treat, provided the flight engineer kept a straight face! Sadly, nowadays this can't happen with flight deck doors securely shut. Back then, it was open house on the captain's invitation!

The second prank was the 'virginity test', played only on crew, for reasons that will become apparent! It involved the captain inviting a stewardess, fresh out of training, to the flight deck for a 'chat'. Picture the scene. A new stewardess, eager to make a good impression, perched on the jump seat in the company of the captain and the rest of the flight deck guys. A very macho environment. The 'test' involved the captain asking the girl about her training, how she liked the job, etc. Then, several questions into the conversation, he would ask if she was a virgin! This always took the girl surprise. If she said "*Yes*" or "*That's none of your business*", the peace on the flight deck was interrupted by the sound of a warning klaxon. Actually, whatever the hapless victim said would result in the klaxon booming out. In the quiet of the night, it made a hell of a racket. At this point, the look on the stewardess' face is easy to imagine. She would have been mortified. Recounting the story here, it all sounds very misogynistic, which it clearly was, but at the time it passed for good natured banter; just another aspect of those bygone times. In today's PC world this wouldn't be tolerated. But as the captain's word was law in those days, they got away with it. Incidentally, it was the flight engineer who, once again, was activating unseen swithes to set the klaxon off!

With all the pranks they were subjected to, I am suprised any of the girls stayed for as long as they did!

5. ISLANDS IN THE SUN

'Seaside Shuffle'
Terry Dactyl & The Dinosaurs

'Weather at our destination is fifty degrees
with some broken clouds, but they'll try to
have them fixed before we arrive.'

The Caribbean destinations were popular on the BOAC network. Barbados, Antigua, St Lucia, Jamaica, Trinidad – my roster read like a travel brochure!

As a new roster arrived through my letterbox, the sense of anticipation, was palpable. But little did I know when my first Caribbean roster landed on the hall carpet that it was to herald the start of a relationship with the area that would span decades.

I loved the Caribbean. Sun drenched sandy beaches swept by the crystal Caribbean waters. Tropical heat. Barefoot beach bars. Fantastically friendly islanders. Irresistible steel band calypso music. The hum of tree frogs and crickets. Brightly coloured humming birds at the breakfast table! So, whenever a roster to that part of the world arrived, I was one happy bunny.

We used to land in the Caribbean mid to late afternoon. After a quick change it was off to the poolside bar to soak up the atmosphere and partake in a Planters Punch, or two! Of all the places we flew to, it was the Caribbean that seemed to me to be worlds away from my life in England. Sure, the Middle East and Far East were also poles apart from life in Blighty but the Caribbean, with its relaxed tropical lifestyle, made me feel I'd arrived on some distant Elysian paradise!

Barbados, with its beautiful red and pink bougainvillea flowers strewn across the island, was one of my favourite layovers. We would spend our time lounging by the pool bar and indulging in the odd bit of water sports. It was a hard life for a twenty-year-old!

Barbados was the only place in the world where I went sick and had to be left behind instead of working my scheduled flight back to London. Going sick necessitated someone else taking my place on the crew. When this happened, it could result in as many as thirty-three other rosters having to be changed. This was because someone had to cover the immediate gap on the flight, then another person had to fill that hole, and so on. For the person reporting sick, all their future rosters were cancelled and a completely new roster given to them. Of course, there were those who played the system to their advantage. If they got a trip they didn't like the look of, they would call in sick. In a heavily unionised environment, this sort of thing went on all the time. But I can honestly say, hand on heart, I never went sick unless it was genuine. It was just one other thing that wasn't in my nature. In fact, I only reported sick twice in the entire time I was crew. This time I had felt unwell when we transited in Antigua, where a check steward reprimanded me for leaning against the door during the turnround. I agree it probably didn't look very professional, but leaning against the door was the only way I was going to remain upright! When I got back to Heathrow, I was hauled in to the Cabin Service Manager to explain myself. I pleaded my case, explaining what happened in Antigua and I was duly found 'not guilty'! They could hardly say otherwise, given I had gone sick at the next layover!

Not all destinations we went to were as welcoming

as Barbados. Like Trinidad. Here we were told not to leave the hotel. Trinidad, in those days, was in the company of places like Washington and Entebbe where we were subject to the same advice. The trouble in Trinidad stemmed from the time of a Black Power protest on the island. A protestor was killed by police and this led to strikes and a partial mutiny in the army. The situation in the early 1970s was still volatile and unstable. As aircrew were a target for all manner of muggers, thugs, and ruffians we had to be careful. Some people did venture out from the upside-down Hilton Hotel in Port of Spain, where you went down from Reception to get to the bedrooms, but I was just as happy to stay put for some authentic Caribbean R&R&R (Rest and Relaxation and Rum!).

Trinidad aside, life in the Caribbean was laid back – almost horizontal. And this rubbed off on us.

The Caribbean was the only part of the world where our standard safety briefings were jazzed up - with a calypso twist. This wasn't something the company required; it was the preserve of a few entertaining first stewards who liked to deliver the briefing as if they were Bob Marley. In true, 'Sorry I Haven't A Clue' tradition, the whole safety briefing was 'sung' to the tune of something like 'Yellow Bird' or 'Day-O'. Here is the actual briefing, so give it a try in your best calypso style!

"In the unlikely event of having to use an escape slide, leave all hand baggage behind and, ladies, remove high heeled shoes. Please now ensure your table is folded away, your seat back upright with the arm rests down, and your seat belt fastened. The seat belt is fastened and adjusted like this, and unfastened like this. Whenever the fasten seat belt signs are on you must return to your seat and fasten your seat belt securely. If for any reason the air supply fails, oxygen will be provided. Masks like this will appear automatically. When you see the masks, remain seated and quickly cover your mouth and nose like this. And breathe normally. Pulling the mask to your face opens the oxygen supply. Do not smoke when oxygen is in use.

Your life jacket is stowed under your seat. When directed to do so by the crew, remove the life jacket from the container and pull it over your head. Pull the tapes down, passing them around your waist and tying them securely in a double bow at the side. To inflate, pull the red toggle. If necessary, the air can be topped up by using this mouthpiece. There is a whistle here for attracting attention. Do not inflate your life jacket until you are outside the aircraft. Junior life jackets are carried for the use of small children."

Even the airline helped with the calypso vibe by serving passengers Rum Swizzlers in colourful BOAC wooden beakers, with the recipe printed on the outside. Potent little things they were too! BOAC also gave passengers a complimentary record on the return journey back to London. The record had tracks like 'Jamaica Farewell', 'Island Woman', and 'Yellow Bird' on it. As a result of all this frivolity, it wasn't at all unusual for slightly squiffy passengers to totter off the plane on arrival at Heathrow which, in keeping with British weather, was usually damp, misty, and grey!

6. AFRICAN SKIES

'You Wear It Well'
Rod Stewart

*'We are pleased to have some of the best flight
attendants in the industry. Unfortunately,
none of them are on this flight.'*

After the North Atlantic trips, the Nairobi /
Johannesburg (Jo'burg) route, with a transit stop in Rome, Frankfurt, Zurich, or
Nicosia, was the route I flew most frequently. On
all these flights we served a main meal on departure from London, which meant we had to get a
wriggle on to get it completed before the transit
stop. Frankfurt was the worst. The flight time was
a mere one hour and twenty minutes, in which

time we had to serve drinks, a meal, and coffee! As the meal had to be heated in the oven for around forty minutes before it could even be served, timings were tight. 'Festina lente' – Latin for 'hurry slowly' – was definitely the watchword for these trips! It made the Bermuda shuttle look like a doddle!

To perform this near impossible feat, the ovens had to be switched on the moment we got on board. This way the food was heating up as passengers were boarding. Which was fine until the flight engineer switched off the galley power. Some did this to make sure they had maximum electrical power to feed critical flight systems for take-off, and they clearly didn't consider an oven to be critical. On such a short flight, I did! To compound the problem, we had to switch the ovens on at intervals of seven minutes, thereby ensuring that the last passengers to get served weren't presented with food that looked like it had come from a crematorium. Preparing the galley for take-off, boarding passengers, dealing with loaders, making coffee, and switching ovens on at specific times, all before you had even left the gate, meant we had to have our wits about us.

Immediately after take-off I would be up and at it, often not waiting for the seat belt signs to be switched off and praying the galley power would be restored if an over keen engineer had switched it off.

Once into the swing of the drinks service, I had to remember to rotate the top two shelves in the oven with the bottom two, which we did after the food had been in for twenty-five minutes. In the middle of a busy drinks service, it was easy to forget this vital manoeuvre. If you did forget, some passengers got hugely overcooked meals and others lukewarm dishes! Yum!

It was a real stretch getting the meals out and then getting the used trays back in before landing. And that was just the first sector. We still had over six hours ahead of us before reaching Nairobi, our first stopover.

The Rome – Nairobi leg wasn't easy for another reason. The meal service was a far more complicated affair than normal. On virtually all our flights, we served a main meal and then either afternoon tea or breakfast to all passengers - everyone got the same menu. But on the Rome – Nairobi flight, things went differently.

Passengers joining the flight at Rome were served open sandwiches with cheese and biscuits on departure. Which was fine. It was breakfast into Nairobi where the fun started. For passengers disembarking there, they were served a full breakfast before arrival, and those passengers going through

to Jo'burg had a continental breakfast. A full breakfast could include the world famous, or should
that be infamous, green omelette. Rubbery in tex-
ture, it came in various disguises! The very first
time I got one of these out of the oven to serve it,
the distinct green tinge was obvious and I immediately thought I'd screwed up, or the loaders had
given us food that was off! I needn't have worried;
it was normal. Every omelette we ever served was
green - and rubbery! Perhaps one of our omelettes
was the reason why Ian Fleming wrote this in his
James Bond short story, '007 in New York':

> 'James Bond, his stomach queasy from the BOAC
> version of an English country house breakfast.
> It was just 10 a.m. on a blue and golden late
> September morning and the BOAC Monarch Flight
> 505 from London had landed at Idlewild...'

Who'd have thought the Beatles and James Bond
had something in common – green omelettes! Omelettes aside, just making sure you had the right
combination of food on board was something of a
challenge. It doesn't sound that complicated when
you write it down, but it was one of those things
that could easily go awry. Give one passenger a full
breakfast when they should have had continental,
and it was good night Vienna for some other poor
soul's stomach!

Our route to Nairobi took us out across the Medi-
terranean to Egypt, then south over Sudan and

Ethiopia. With Nairobi located eighty-eight miles south of the Equator, all flights had to cross this invisible line. Due to the proximity of Nairobi to the Equator, we were more or less on our final approach when we crossed it. Because of this, there wasn't much we could do to mark the occasion, as ships do when they 'cross the line'. Back in the 1950s, BOAC gave passengers certificates confirming their first Equator crossing, but this practice had long since ended by the time I first crossed it. In the world of aviation, we needed to be a bit more creative. Some captains, as the aircraft passed over the Equator, would give the control column a quick pull/push movement, making the plane 'bump'. As they did this, they announced the plane had just crossed the Equator. The same thing was also done crossing the International Date Line in the Pacific. Passengers loved it!

When we got to Nairobi, the simple task of getting from the airport to the hotel was often fraught with problems and not that simple. East African Airways handled BOAC on the ground in Nairobi. By any standard, EAA were something of a ragtag outfit run on a shoestring. We would often arrive and then have to wait while they found a driver, found a vehicle, or both! Once, we even had to have a whip round to give them the money to buy fuel for the bus. They simply didn't have the cash to put petrol in the tank! Interestingly, EAA went bust five years later with debts in excess of US$120.million and the main shareholders, Uganda, Kenya and Tanzania, set about forming their own seperate international airlines in the process.

Nairobi was the only place where I ended up in hospital, albeit only for an out-patient visit. I had suffered a bout of neuralgia on the flight for which the chief steward had adminsitered his home spun remedy, brown milk. Brown milk was hot milk generously laced with brandy, which you used to wash down two aspirins. It worked a treat and I got through the flight without bother. Despite this, the chief steward insisted I went to hospital to get myself checked over. So, off I trot to Nairobi General. Compared to an NHS hospital, it was pretty basic, but it was clean and the staff friendly. That day, I wasn't the only walking wounded crew member; one of the girls had suffered abdominal pain on the same flight!

After getting checked over by the doc, he said I was free to leave and carry on as normal. My companion, on the other hand, wasn't so lucky. She had to stay in and was determined unfit to fly when we left for Jo'burg the next day. I don't know what happened to her after that – presumably a passenger ride home and a whole set of new rosters into the bargain!

Later that day, I was sufficiently recovered to pay a visit to the hotel bar where I ran into a middle-

aged English lady and exchanged a few pleasantries. I assumed, given her age and appearance, she
was an expat who welcomed the chance of a chat
with someone from 'back home'. How wrong I was!

After chatting for a time about everything and
nothing, she said she thought I may be able to help
her with some family 'business'. The 'business'
turned out to be the job of taking a package across
the border into neighbouring Tanzania! She didn't
specify the contents but I guessed it may be gold,
or possibly a bundle of illegal, undeclared cash.
Currency restrictions on money leaving Kenya,
strictly enforced at the time, meant people had to
find other ways to get their cash out of the country before the government claimed it for their own
Swiss bank accounts.

She had it all worked out. The plan was that I
would use her car to drive a package across the
border and then meet up with a bloke who would
take the package off my hands. In return, I was to
get paid five hundred pounds! Yeh, right! Anything
involving that amount of money clearly came with
a high level of risk. I wasn't about to agree to the
mad cap scheme. The fact she wasn't prepared to
do it herself, that I was a total stranger to her, that
she hadn't divulged what the contents were, all
made me think I would, most likely, end up dead
in a ditch as soon as I handed the package over. Or
inside a Kenyan or Tanzanian goal – which didn't

appeal to me one bit!

That she made the approach wasn't as odd as it may first appear. It was possible she had heard the stories about BOAC stewards who, in the past, had been involved in smuggling. In one case in the Fifties, a former steward appeared as a witness in a diamond smuggling case against several other stewards. The diamonds, worth fourteen thousand pounds in total, were smuggled on flights between London and New York. One steward admitted the offence, turning Queens Evidence to avoid a prison sentence. Another steward went to prison for two years for his smuggling activities. BOAC aircrew were also caught up in a big way in the gold smuggling rackets that existed in India and Pakistan during the 1950s and 1960s. It was no secret that BOAC sacked a great number of stewards in an attempt to stamp the practice out! Maybe, she thought we were all cut from the same cloth!

Guess what? I didn't take her up on her kind offer and was pleased to be on my way to Johannesburg the next day! Had I done done what she wanted, I might well have ended up fulfilling the Port Said prediction - or worse!

After the encounter, I never saw her again in the Panafric, which was our crew hotel in Nairobi. Maybe she had done the job herself – who knows! Maybe she was the one who ended up face down in a ditch?

The flight from Nairobi down to Jo'burg took three hours forty minutes. With its sprawling Soweto township, Johannesburg was unlike anywhere else we flew to and this was because of apartheid. In Afrikaans, apartheid means 'apart-hood'. The apartheid policy placed restrictions on people based on the colour of their skin. People were classified into four main groups: White, Black, Indian, and Coloured. A person's classification depended on a range of ridiculous tests the government made people take. For example, if someone could hold a pencil in their hair while shaking their head, they were not white!

If a person was classified as white, they could move around freely, go where they wanted. If a person was classified as non-white, they could only use places designated for 'blacks and coloureds'. This manifested itself in everyday life. Black only bus stops. Black only hospitals. White only beaches. Segregated swimming pools. Black only park benches. Trains, toilets, even burial grounds - all segregated.

It was the law, and we encountered it whenever we stepped out of our hotel. On one occasion I stopped at a shop to buy a snack where there was a long line of black people waiting, so I joined the back of the queue – as I would do back home. The shopkeeper spotted me and, over the heads of those queuing, indicated for me to come up to the counter. Looking back, I am not proud of the fact that I followed his instruction and got served immediately. But there were far worse indignities than having to queue and wait in line to be served meted out to the black population.

Black people could be whipped for standing in a 'whites only' doorway, and black people were treated like cattle. The trains showed this to be true. Trains had six or so 'white only' carriages, with just a couple of carriages at the rear of the train for non-whites. While 'white only' carriages had a handful of people in them, the black carriages were full beyond capacity. People had to sit on the roof or hang off the outside because they couldn't get inside. As I experienced on a train to Pretoria one trip, it felt very wrong being in a virtually empty 'white only' carriage, watching the squalor of Soweto pass by the window, while its inhabitants were clinging on to the roof of the train.

Despite apartheid, we did have fun in Jo'burg and, because of the general situation there, room parties featured heavily on the entertainment schedule! Most of these parties involved sitting around chatting, having a laugh, relaxing with a beer. I never saw a single game of spin the bottle, or room keys thrown into a hat! Wild stories of tequila filled romps with captains licking salt from a stewardess's navel, girls gyrating on tables, and folk in bed together passed me by. Clearly, I wasn't invited to those parties!

But one Jo'burg party does stand out. And that was because it was the one and only time in my life when I went anywhere in drag. Dressed as a stewardess!

I have no idea who came up with the idea, I think it was one of the girls on my crew. They thought it would be a giggle to dress me in one of their uniforms and give me a plausible cover story about just arriving off a flight and going straight to the party without changing first. What possessed me to agree is beyond me. It certainly wasn't out of any burning ambition to put a frock on!

I enjoyed the getting ready bit. It was great fun, in my boxers, being dressed by the girls! And it was hilarious! Me struggling into the dress was a wonder to behold. And then came the hair and makeup. By the time they had finished with me, I looked the part and, worryingly, I made a passable, if not all that attractive, 'bird'! The only problem was I couldn't fit into any of their shoes so I had to carry them, claiming my feet were sore from the flight in!

It was a good party and I must have made an impression. Only a couple of people there rumbled

I was a bloke! In the end, I left the party early. This was because another steward, three sheets to the wind, took a lecherous shine to me. I made a very swift exit; not to do so meant someone was definitely going to get more than they bargained for! But I had learnt a valuable life lesson. I now appreciated what a woman goes through to get ready for a night out, and what a pain a drunk bloke can be! One thing is certain, not many stewards can say they have worn the famous little pink number that was the Clive uniform! In fairness, it might be more than I think!

For my part, I was no drag queen. Just a bloke dressed up in a frock for a laugh!

****

Rostering should have given crew variety in where they went, but I spent a disproportionate amount of my time in Africa. Why that was, I have no idea. Luck of the draw perhaps, or someone in Crew Reporting had taken against me!

In addition to my regular jaunts down to Jo'burg, I also got to fly to less salubrious places in Africa like Lagos and Entebbe.

Lagos wasn't even on the BOAC route map. BOAC had flown to Lagos in the past, but they relinquished the route to British Caledonian the year I joined. The fact that I flew to Lagos at all was pure chance.

A Nigerian Airways flight had gone tech at Heathrow, so BOAC stepped in and provided a plane and crew to operate the service. This arrangement was a leftover from the 1960s when BOAC operated VC10 services to Lagos, on behalf of Nigerian Airways.

I was on standby so got the call to take the eight-hour flight to Lagos, via Kano. Standby was a tedious business. There were three levels of standby. In each case, we had to be able to get to the airport within that time. We started on a twelve-hour standby, meaning we had to be able to report for duty within twelve hours of being called in. If we survived the twelve-hour slot, we moved up to the four-hour standby. If we weren't called during this period, we moved on to the dreaded one-and-a-half-hour standby. If we survived this and didn't get called, we took our next scheduled rostered flight. It was entirely possible to have a great trip scheduled after your standby, only to miss it by being called out during your standby. On this occasion, I should have been going to Nicosia – which was a really easy working day – not a hell hole like Lagos!

The flight down was easy as we had the Nigerian

crew to help with the cabin service. But I could have done without them regaling us with doom laden stories about the various Nigerian Airways' disasters that had happened over the years, all involving the type of aircraft we were on! They told us about the VC10 that had crashed two years before on landing in Lagos, killing all eighty-seven people on board. Good to know! They also told the tale of the VC10 that landed there in 1966 and was immediately hijacked by local rebels. At the time, the rebels were attempting a coup d'état in which they murdered the Head of State and replaced him with one of the conspirators. After getting the fare paying passengers off, the rebels used the VC10 to fly their families out of Lagos to safety in Kano. After that, they did, to their credit, return the plane and release the crew.

Despite these tales, nothing quite prepared me for my first encounter with Nigeria. In 1971, Nigeria was recovering from a brutal civil war. More commonly called the Biafran War, which had only ended the year before I flew there. The war had racked the country for three years, bringing untold horrors down on its population. The Biafrans took the brunt of the savagery, with up to two million dying of starvation through the course of the conflict. In the inevitable vacuum that followed the end of the conflict, a faltering government did little to stop the civil violence that filled the void with, especially, extremely ruthless armed gangs roaming freely across the capital terrorising all who lived and worked there.

As we travelled in the crew bus from the airport through the city to our hotel, the route took us along the seafront - with the city's buildings on the right-hand side and Bar Beach on the other. It was the beach that grabbed my attention.

In an attempt to regain order and quell the street violence, the government had introduced some very harsh measures. What had got my attention on the beach were the posts driven into the sand near the water's edge. This was where people were publicly executed by firing squad. The day before, a notorious armed robber had been shot in a public spectacle that drew a crowd of around thirty thousand people! For me, a twenty-year-old straight out of Britain, the fact this was entertainment for the masses was way beyond my ability to absorb and comprehend. With capital punishment abolished in Britain, this felt savage and brutal in the extreme, and a reminder of just what life in Nigeria was really like. It was definitely not a safe place to take in the sites.

If the ride along the beach was shocking, arrival at the hotel heralded a more comical turn of events!

The Maryland Guest House was not our usual standard of hotel, having been found at short notice to accommodate us on this unscheduled trip. It was a peculiar mix of Fawlty Towers meets shanty town, which was all too obvious on entering my room.

A quick check of the bed confirmed my worst fears about the place! As I pulled the top sheets back, I found the bottom sheet was heavily stained! With what I don't know. It had been laundered, but there was no way was I going to sleep in it. Despite the sweltering heat the room had no aircon. Instead of an aircon unit, there was only a large hole in the wall. To make matters worse, the hole was at ground level. An open invitation for anything that crawled or slithered to pay me a visit. It was definitely the sort of place where I banged my shoes together to ensure no unwelcome creature had found its way in. In this case, top of my list for unwanted visitors were Great African land snails. Eaten as snacks in Nigerian bars, these beasties are big and can be as long as eight inches and as tall as three. I grant you, I might have seen one in my shoe anyway, but I was taking no chances as they carried meningitis! And, if Billy Connolly is to be believed, Nigerian snails can crawl up your bum and raise a family inside you! Now do you see why I was so worried about my hole - the one in the wall, I mean!

I decided I needed to change my room and as there was no phone, I headed for Reception. As I came out into the corridor, I met one of the girls emerging from her room and, from the description she gave, it was clear changing rooms wouldn't solve anything. So we gave up on the idea of going to Reception and headed for the bar instead. There we ran into another 'room refugee' from our crew with much the same tale of woe. We proceeded to drown our sorrows with the local brew, Star Lager. To cut a long story short, I got ratted and the girls didn't! What they knew, which I didn't, was that the lager contained high levels of glycerin, added to the beer as a preservative in Africa and India. The girls 'strained' the beer through clenched teeth as they drank. This, supposedly, mitigates the potency the glycerin gives the brew. Anyway, sometime later that day, they poured me back into my room - which was in exactly the same state as I had left it! I have less than edifying recollections of talking down the throne trumpet that night!

I owe the fact that I got up at all for the flight home the next day to the girls. Concerned for my welfare, they knocked on my door to get me up. No doubt about it, they were good to me. Not only did they make sure I was up and that I made it on to the crew bus, but they also let me snooze all the way on the internal leg of the flight between Lagos to Kano! Of course, there were rules about drinking alcohol and operating a flight. From 'bottle to throttle' we had to have be a break of eight hours, which I complied with by minutes! I never got that wasted down the routes ever again! Lesson leant!

Another lousy African trip was to Entebbe in Uganda, an alternative BOAC route down to Jo'burg. My first trip there was a couple of months after Idi Amin seized power in a military coup. The coup involved an attack on Entebbe airport, during which two priests were shot dead. The bullet holes in the terminal walls that greeted us were a graphic witness to the attack.

It's not known how many people died under Amin's regime; but estimates put it as high as five hundred thousand. In the early 1970s the brutality was at its beginning. Reports of beatings and abductions were growing by the day. Gang rape was a trademark of the thugs who were Amin supporters and who Amin used to 'influence' people toward his way of thinking. As a consequence, we were advised to stay in our hotel and not venture out. It was sound advice. Gangs prowled the streets armed with clubs, with nails stuck in the end for extra nastiness. They were not people I personally ever wanted to encounter, so I stayed put in the hotel.

****

One aspect of flying in Africa, and the Far East for that matter, were the number of unaccompanied minors we carried. These were children, travelling without their parents, flying to and from boarding schools in England. Some travelled as unaccompanied minors, travelling alone, others were chaperoned by an 'auntie'. An 'auntie' was a stewardess whose sole job was to look after the little darlings. Aunties travelled as passengers, so weren't directly part of the crew. Stewards, thank heavens, were never entrusted with the task!

The kids would be enrolled into the BOAC Junior Jet Club and, on being awarded their membership, they received a log book and a metal 'wings' badge. On most flights, they also got to visit the flight deck where the captain would sign their log book with an entry for the flight. For many, these log books were, and remain, prized possessions.

How ever they were travelling, they weren't immune from me playing the odd prank on them! I'd tell them to look out the window for winged dinosaurs, flying broomsticks, or even Santa - at Christmas time! Guess what, not a winged dinosaur, flying broomstick, or Santa were ever sighted!

7. YELLOW BRICK ROAD

'Ride A White Swan'

T Rex

*'We will be serving dinner on our flight this evening.
And ice cream if everybody behaves themselves.'*

A typical round trip to Australia would take anything up to twenty-one days, slipping in the Middle East, India, and the Far East. A stop could be a single night, or it could be as long as several days!

There were many routes going east. Some involved a transit or night stop in Europe in Frankfurt, Zurich, or Rome; others made their first stop in the Middle East in Beirut, Doha, Dubai, or Kuwait.

After that, it was on to the Subcontinent, via Bombay (now Mumbai), Delhi, Calcutta (now Kolkata), or Karachi.

Then you headed off to Oz, by way of Singapore, Hong Kong, Bangkok, or Rangoon (now Yangon). We made landfall in Australia in Darwin or Perth, before reaching the end point of the trip, Sydney or Melbourne.

Much of the time, we flew direct to Beirut from London. To a lot of people, Beirut was a great place for a slip. I didn't share that view! Beirut's glory days of the 1950s and 1960s were well in the past. Back in those days, Hollywood 'A' listers frequented the city - a fashionable destination to be seen in. By the time I got there that had all but gone.

Crews still talk about the great times they had shopping in Beirut and of whiling away hours in the Golden Bar, but that wasn't the Beirut I found.

I found a city with dark undertones. As one taxi driver put it, *"Beirut is like a rose. Very beautiful, but its thorns are sharp."* The story of Deborah Thornton Jackson, no relation, perfectly illustrates how true this was. Jackson was a one-time BOAC stewardess who found fame in 1971 as the 'Anytime, Anyplace, Anywhere' Martini girl. One year later she headed out to Beirut to help a friend who had run into bad company and ended up herself falling in with the wrong crowd. After being drugged in a bar one evening, she was coerced into working as a 'hostess' in a bar-cum-brothel called the Crazy Horse Saloon. Jackson's passport was stolen and her money taken, effectively rendering her a prisoner. She was 'rescued' by a local Lebanese playboy who 'bought' her and married her. In the seventeen years she remained in Beirut she endured the civil war – living some of the time in the basement of her home. With the help of Dutch mercenaries, she eventually fled the city and made it back to Europe. In many ways, her fall from the glamorous lifestyle she once had was an appropriate metaphor for what had happened to Beirut itself.

As well as its decline from chic, through seedy to deadly dangerous, the city in 1972 was starting to reveal the tensions that would lead to full scale civil war four years later. These tensions, the internecine conflict between Phalangists and Palestinians, were spilling over into everyday life. From time to time, gunfire crackled across squares and streets in downtown Beirut. The most at-risk areas were the port and the uptown streets with their fashionable shops and our crew hotel, the Bristol!

Hijacking was becoming a constant threat to flights in and out of the city. In 1970, Pan Am Flight 93 was hijacked from Beirut and flown to

Cairo, where the plane was blown up. In the same year, Beirut was the next scheduled stop for BOAC Flight 775 when it was unceremoniously hijacked to Dawson's Field. More on that later.

Against this background I still went sightseeing! After all, I was travelling to see the world and not just hotel swimming pools!

Along with one of our stewardesses, Margaret, we headed for Byblos, now a UNESCO World Heritage Site. Byblos is thought to be one of the oldest continually inhabited places in the world and a key military camp for the Crusaders on their way to and from the Holy Land. The tour offered a discount for married couples, so Margaret and I decided we would go along as husband and wife. Which was to sow the seeds of a comical incident the following day. On the tour we got chatting to a couple who were on holiday and, to keep up the discount pretense, we didn't let on about not being married! Next day, as we were on the plane preparing for departure, who should come up the steps but the very same couple. They were really pleased, and surprised, to see us and thought it was sweet and fantastic that we could travel the world working together! Little did they know that had we been married Margaret would have had to have left the job! We never let on!

Despite the threatening nature of the place, in the

end the worst thing that happened to me in Beirut was that the hotel lost my laundry! Not the end of the world I grant you, but the loss of my white jackets would have been a hanging offence! At the eleventh hour, the hotel redeemed themselves and found my laundry, presenting it to me as we boarded the crew bus at 01.30, much to the amusement of the rest of the crew.

After Beirut it was on to one of the Gulf States: Kuwait, Bahrain, Doha, Abu Dhabi, or Dubai.

Of all of these, Kuwait was by far the most developed. Unlike most other Gulf States, Kuwait actively embraced liberal Western attitudes and it was not uncommon to see Kuwaiti women wearing mini-skirts, rather than hijabs. By contrast, Dubai was a far less liberal state and, although its economy was booming from the Middle East's oil boom, high-rise hotels and apartment blocks were yet to be built there. When I went there it was little more than a small town, with ancient dhows ploughing up and down the city's creek.

Dubai's airport was only seven miles from RAF Sharjah; their runways running parallel to one another. There was a story of a BOAC VC10 landing at Sharjah by mistake. In fairness, this was not a problem unique to Dubai. In 1960, a Pan Am 707 had managed to mistake RAF Northolt for Heathrow and landed there! The RAF were not amused, so the two large gasometers on the approach to Heathrow were painted 'NO' for Northolt, and 'LH' for Heathrow. Now at least, pilots had a visual reference point for the direction they should be headed!

I enjoyed exploring the souks of Dubai. Nothing more than a collection of alleyways and small shops crammed in side by side, the souks had their own magic. At every turn, there were men huddled around hookahs (hubble-bubble pipes) playing board games and peddlers trying to sell a carpet or two. Some followed us around like flies stuck to fly-paper. It was as if we had a neon sign flashing 'BOAC' on our forehead, marking us out as potential targets! In fairness, we didn't need a neon sign, we stuck out like sore thumbs anyway and probably looked a very easy touch!

On one trip there we touched down for a night stop only to be told we weren't going anywhere soon. A catering strike at Heathrow had stopped flights from reaching us. Such was the power of the in-flight meal!

With no flights we sat around the hotel pool sunbathing. All we were told to do was wait. So, day after day we lounged by the pool and worked on the tan. But that held its own dangers as the company took a dim view of crew turning up for a flight with sunburned, peeling faces! As the manual said, *"A peeled and swollen face is unattractive and quite unacceptable"*. I get their reasoning!

As luck would have it our captain had served in the RAF with the Station Commander of RAF Sharjah that resulted in us being invited to spend evenings on the base. This was a great idea and I loved it. It was a touch surreal to be sat in an RAF base, in the middle of the desert, watching films under the stars in an open-air cinema!

As well as watching movies, we also enjoyed betting on camel spider races, the Arabian equivalent of snail racing! About the size of a cigarette packet, camel spiders were fearsome looking critters. Although harmless, they scared the life out of any unsuspecting soul when they leapt in the air and grabbed hold of a trouser leg! It happened to me. Seriously, not funny! Predictably, the rest of the crew thought it hysterical!

Like everywhere else in the Gulf, the big attraction for the servicemen were our girls. Which bought its own benefits. First, we got to have fun at the base rather than endure yet another room party. Second, the girls stuck close to us stewards in order to ward off any unwanted attention. Tough job, but someone had to do it!

When the strike finally ended a Standard VC10 turned up to take us back to Blighty. On the Standard, my crew seat was half way down the cabin by the door and, unlike all the other planes we worked on, I sat on my own in what I termed the 'Billy-no-mates' seat! The stewardess, who would normally sit with me, was also on her own down the back.

The day we finally left was a typical hot desert day. But immediately we took off I sensed something wasn't right. We were climbing, but weren't gaining height as we normally did. This felt anything but a normal departure.

When I heard the engines throttle back, I began to fret. Engines throttling back would be standard noise abatement procedure over a built-up area like a city, but over the desert? And that low? I didn't imagine we were doing it to avoid upsetting Bedouin camels and livestock! A quick glance out of the small window in the door confirmed my worst fears. Not only were we not climbing, we were now descending toward the desert sand. That wasn't right and it wasn't good. So, I checked the 'No Smoking' signs. When these went off it meant that all flight systems were normal and the take-off was fine and usually they went off almost immediately after take-of. But not today; something was definitely amiss.

It looked for all the world as though we were heading for a repeat performance of the stricken

Hermes all those years earlier. What really baffled me was the absence of any warnings about trouble from the flight deck. Given we were about to crash, my attention turned, with dread, to the escape slide - the very type I broke in training! The desert floor kept on getting closer. At the point where it was about to become a brown trousers job, we stopped descending. We weren't climbing, but at least we were no longer heading down. Airborne was good – even if it was a tad low. After a brief pause, the engines roared back to life and we started climbing again – properly this time. The receding desert floor was a welcome sight! At least, I wasn't going to be tested against the slide this day.

As it turned out, nothing had been wrong. We had 'only' 'buzzed' RAF Sharjah! In a classic comms cock-up, no one had thought to tell me the plan for our departure! The flight deck, the rest of the crew, even the passengers, knew but I was in blissful ignorance! The base was due to close later that year, so our captain decided it would be a nice idea to do a fly-past over the base; his way of saying thank you for their hospitality and saluting the work of the base over the years. Hence, the descent immediately after take-off.

It must have been an impressive sight. With a full load of passengers onboard we had roared down the runway at a little over one-hundred feet before making a steep climb out. An air show manoeuvre, with a commercial passenger plane, on a scheduled flight!

The taciturn response from the Control Tower to our display was: "*Not bad for civilians!*" High praise indeed coming from the RAF! I later discovered the VC10 was one of the most maneuverable planes ever built. It could execute low level passes, like the one we performed, because 'ground effect', the thing that makes it dangerous for other planes to fly this low, was almost nonexistent. Mind you, one hundred feet was low enough for me! Six years after this little escapade a VC10, captained by Tony Smith, flew down the runway at a White Waltham airshow at a mere twenty feet! What is the saying RAF pilots use for low level flying: '*If you can see the legs of the cows, you're OK. If you can see the legs of the sheep, you're too low!*'

****

When we were in the Gulf, we did all the usual sightseeing trips crew do. Riding on camels, lunching in Bedouin tents (feasting on sheep's eye balls), or sailing on a dhow. Dhows are the traditional sailing vessel of the region, used for all purposes such as fishing and carrying cargo. And, as in our case, tourist trips. The dhows were interesting, mainly because of the 'thunder box'. The 'thunder box' was basically a box hanging out over the sea at the stern. It was the local seagoing version of a loo. Inside the box there was a hole in the floor and, apparently, a splendid view of the sea! Didn't fancy it. Waited until I got back to the hotel! Apart from anything else, the pitching of the boat from side to side would have made it an unpleasant and, highly possibly, a mucky experience to say the least!

During Gulf layovers, we often got invited to parties by divers working in the offshore oil business. Once again, the girls were the attraction. We stewards went along for the free drinks, and to provide the girls with an excuse to leave at the end of the evening! At these gatherings the chic choice of music was stuff like 'Nights in White Satin' or 'A Whiter Shade of Pale'. T-Rex tracks also featured frequently. I assume divers thought this might turn the girls' love lights on! With plenty of booze flowing, we always had a great time - but I don't remember an evening when we didn't come home with all the girls!

What made partying in the region all the more remarkable was that most places were 'dry'. Alcohol was banned in most states and transgression of their religious law was not something the authorities took lightly! Yet, being a resourceful lot, or just very needy for a drink, we devised ways to get round the law!

First, we had to get the booze off the plane and to

the hotel without getting caught! So a degree of subterfuge was employed. One resourceful flight engineer came up with the idea of hiding a small length of hosepipe in his hat, with a cork in each end, filled with his favourite tipple. Because customs officers never checked inside crew hats in those days, he got away with it! Another gambit involved a bottle opening and re-sealing gizmo which could be purchased in the local flea market. It took caps off tonic water bottles without damaging the cap, meaning it could be resealed and the tonic water replaced with vodka or gin. The device made such a good job it was impossible to detect the bottle had been tampered with. Some of the crew's white jacket cover bags clanked something wicked as they came off the aircraft, and ever so gently carried past Customs. To be fair, most of the time the Custom guys we encountered were either half asleep or utterly disinterested - usually both!

Having got the drink to the hotel, we then had to consume it discreetly. Room parties were one way, another involved taking a teapot off the aircraft which we then filled with white wine 'liberated' from first-class. This then made its way to the restaurant for dinner where we consumed the contents from teacups in full view of the other diners. It worked, to all intent and purposes we were drinking tea!

Tehran, the capital of Iran, was one of the most

relaxed and liberal of all the Arab cities we flew to and it had some quirky characteristics that set it apart from the rest. Unusually, the city sported loads of roundabouts – normally the preserve of the English road system. The roundabouts were a feature of the elegant tree lined roads that fanned out across the city, many sporting impressive fountains, ponds and lush green lawns at their centre. The Shah, an avid Anglophile, even had red and white double decker style London buses for the metropolis' public transport network. What with these and the roundabouts, the city had a comforting and familiar air to it. What wasn't so familiar was the traffic. The roads were packed with Paykans - aka the Iranian Chariot! This was the country's equivalent of the VW Beetle, a car for the people, of which there were also quite a few! In another nod to the British, the Paykan was a replica of a great British institution, the Rootes Group's Hillman Hunter car. But what set Tehran apart from the other places we went to were not these English influences, or the urbane elegance and relaxed attitudes of its people, but the way the locals drove.

It was near suicidal.

Take intersections, for example. The technique to get across one of these was pure madness. As cars approached the intersection, no matter how busy it was, instead of slowing down to proceed with caution they floored the accelerator and rocketed towards it, foot flat to the floor going as fast as the old jalopies could manage. It was standard practice. With no traffic lights to check their progress, cars hurtled across the crossroads at break neck speed. There was no slowing down at all. It was a form of motorised chicken! The theory was the faster you go, the quicker you got across the junction – so the safer you were. Insane! I have never seen so many cars at the side of the road that ended up on the wrong end of that particular manoeuvre. For us it wasn't that bad because we travelled from the airport into the city in a crew minibus. Still, it was something else to experience first-hand crossing a major intersection in this fashion. Somehow, at speeds that would make your toes curl, and more by luck than judgement, we always made it safely across. That said, I always felt safer in a BOAC jet at 30,000 feet than I ever did in an Iranian minibus!

It was on a flight out of Tehran that I experienced what it's like to be on a plane when someone claims they have put a bomb onboard!

On this particular flight, we were cruising at 37,000 feet about half-way into our three-hour flight to Tel Aviv. We were cruising high above the pure white clouds that floated gently in an ice-blue sky above an empty desert. The cabin glowed with a soft pale blue light from the ceiling bulbs mingling with the sunlight streaming in through the windows. With alternate red and blue seats sporting fresh white antimacassars, the aircraft looked beautiful and the atmosphere was calm and sophisticatedly quiet. There was no hint of what was about to unfold.

I was in the rear galley when the intercom buzzed, calling us to the forward galley. This only ever meant one thing – and change of plan, a problem with the plane, or trouble of some sort at our destination but a divert due to a technical fault was my first thought.

Gathered together in the forward galley, the chief steward told us about the situation. A bomb threat had been telephoned to our Tehran office, where staff were busily assessing the credibility of the threat. The captain had already started looking for possible airports where we could land in order to get the passengers, and ourselves, safely off the aircraft.

Diverting to an airport in Iraq or Jordan was not that appealing. Neither country was on good terms diplomatically with Iran where we had come from, and the fact that we were heading for Israel meant we could expect less than an open-arms welcome. It was for this reason, that whenever we flew into Tel Aviv our passports were never stamped because other Arab countries would have refused us entry! It was also a possibility that the threat was designed to get us to land where we could be held hostage. Far-fetched? We didn't think so. First, because state sponsored terrorism was a reality in the region at the time. Second, one of our VC10s, flying in exactly the same part of the world, had been hijacked only months earlier and flown, at pistol point, to an airfield in Jordan.

BOAC Flight 775 had departed Bahrain en-route to Beirut when Palestine terrorists seized it. The plane was forced to fly to a small airstrip called Dawson's Field in Jordan where it joined a Swissair plane and a TWA plane hijacked five days earlier. Dawson's Field, renamed by the terrorists as 'Revolutionary Airport', was an old RAF base. The aim of the terrorists was to swop the hostages for prisoners – such as Leila Khaled.

Khaled, a member of the Popular Front for the Liberation of Palestine, a terrorist organisation, was being held by Britain for her part in the hijacking of an El Al flight in 1970. During the hijack attempt, her accomplice was shot by sky-marshals and the plane, flying from Amsterdam to New York, diverted into Heathrow where Khalid was arrested immediately the plane landed. Khaled was also part of the team that hijacked a TWA plane between Rome and Tel Aviv in 1969. In that incident, they blew the plane up on the ground after setting the passengers and crew free.

In the Dawson's Field hijack, passengers and crew were held at the improvised desert airfield for three days. In a message smuggled out of the camp, Captain Cyril Goulbourn, pilot of the captured plane, said in the scribbled message, *"Conditions are very crowded. Some people are in constant fear. All BOAC passengers and crew are in good spirits and high morale but please get us out as soon as possible as each passing day things become more difficult."*

I cannot imagine what it must have been like to be held under those circumstances; not knowing if you would ever get out alive. Thankfully, it had a happy ending. The hostages were freed unharmed in return for Khaled's freedom, but the terrorists still blew all the planes up!

On hearing the news of the possible bomb, our first steward, Brent, went visibly pale. Incredibly, he had been one of the stewards hijacked to Dawson's Field. Needless to say, he didn't take the news well. At least we only had a bomb to deal with. Only a bomb? Compared to the hijack Brent went through, where terrorists armed with grenades and pistols stormed the flight deck, we only had a bomb!

Although the person telephoning the threat had said the bomb was in one of the hold bags, our first instinct was to search the plane. But we didn't. If the information in the call was accurate, then a search would have been pointless. Anyway, what would we do if we found it? We could hardly chuck it out the window!

Looking down the length of the serene cabin, with passengers blissfully unaware of the developing situation, everything looked normal. Yet in seconds we could be vaporised into a million fragments. Although this was definitely a 'squeaky bum' moment, I was calm and detached about it all. It isn't until something like this happens that a person knows how they will react. Against all my expectations, I kept it together by consoling myself with the fact that since Brent was on board, lightning was unlikely to strike the same place twice! I know that's a flawed way of looking at it because of people like Roy Sullivan. Sullivan was a US Park Ranger who had been stuck by lightening no less than seven times and had survived to tell the tale. But I still held on to the belief we were going to be OK! Fifteen very long minutes passed before the news came through from the ground that the call had been assessed as a probable hoax so I returned to the rear galley, hoping the guys on the ground were right. I had noted the use of the word 'probable'!

With the excitement behind us, we continued on our merry way to Tel Aviv, landing without further incident. The office guys had made the right call and we duly headed for the hotel bar to celebrate our survival! I had no idea then I would end up later in life working in counter terrorism assessing bomb threats and dealing with suspect packages on a fairly regular basis - walking towards suspect packages whilst telling others to get as far away as possible!

Although this was the only bomb threat I experienced in my time with BOAC, they were not uncommon. It was part and parcel of flying through the 'golden age of hijacking'! During my time as a steward, there were a total of twenty-two planes hijacked worldwide, three of which were destroyed by bombs. One hundred and ten people died in these outrages. Even in the month I finished my training, a BOAC plane from London to Khartoum was forced by fighter jets to land in Libya. On board was Sudanese rebel leader Babiker El Nur. El Nur had been proclaimed Sudan's president in a coup the previous week. There were twenty-six English school children on the flight and, as soon as they were on the ground, El Nur and his companion were taken off the plane. Within the week, both were executed. The plane was eventually released to return to Heathrow safely, where everyone onboard disembarked unharmed.

Four weeks later, a BOAC 747 flying from Montreal to London got diverted to Colorado, due to a bomb threat. The Jumbo travelled over three thousand miles out of its way to land in Denver because it was thought the bomb was a barometric pressure device, primed to explode at an altitude somewhere under five thousand feet, making Denver an ideal place to land as the airport there is at an elevation of over 5,000 feet. One thing was certain, there was one item of kit BOAC had forgotten to issue to me, and that was a tin helmet!

That bomb scare wasn't the only thing that ever happened to me on trips to Israel. One time, I was sitting with some of the crew at a small pavement cafe close to the crew hotel in Tel Aviv. After conducting the usual post mortem on the flight, our attention turned to planning a sightseeing trip to Jerusalem, Bethlehem, Jericho, and the Dead Sea. We wanted to do the trip as a whole crew, so we had to find a way to persuade our two delightful Chinese girls to join us. Shy and wary of our extrovert Western ways, particularly with alcohol, getting them to join in wasn't guaranteed. It was normal for us to have one national girl on a crew; but this trip we had two because one was flying as a supernumerary.

As we discussed the best way to convince them to come along, we were approached by a slightly disheveled looking Arab woman. Wearing multiple layers of clothes, she reminded me of the gypsy women we used to see on the streets of

Britain trying to sell sprigs of lucky heather. We brushed her first overtures away, but she persisted and decided to work on me - I must have looked the most gullible amongst us! I declined her offer, but she persisted. I declined again. When she tried a third time, somewhat appropriate given the biblical connections of where we were, I ignored her.

The next thing I know she's standing behind me ranting about something or other, pointing at me. Most animated. As none of us spoke her language, we didn't have a clue what she was saying. I decided the best policy was to hide behind my beer glass and keep shtum. How very British. It was only when the cafe's owner intervened and sent her packing that we discovered what had been said. As we hadn't bought anything from her, she'd put a curse on me! Of course, I disregarded it as stuff and nonsense and it was soon forgotten. But I have to confess, there have been times in my life when things have gone totally pear-shaped, when I have wondered if there was something to that 'curse'!

The next day, with our Chinese girls in tow, we set off for a day's sightseeing. In Jerusalem we visited the Wailing Wall, the Mount of Olives and the Garden of Gethsemane at the foot of the Mount. We saw the ruined walls of Jericho, went down into the grotto at the Church of the Nativity in Bethlehem and drove out into the Judaean Desert. The final stop on our whistle-stop tour was the Dead Sea, the lowest point on Earth.

At the Dead Sea, only me, the first steward and the Chinese girls wanted to swim. For stewardesses known for their shy, reserved nature, the fact they were happy to be seen in a swimming costume was a surprise. After changing we bought ourselves a cup of tea, a vital prop for our impending salty dip! Known as the Salt Sea, or the Sea of Death, the Dead Sea is one of the Earth's most unique locations. It is the saltiest body of water in the world, ten times saltier than the oceans, which is said to give it restorative health properties. But we weren't there for our health; we just wanted to experience the water's buoyancy. Because the water is hypersaline, we bobbed around on the surface as if we were sitting in a chair at home – our cup of tea floating on its saucer beside us. Everything floats in that water, nothing sinks. Because of that, it was an extraordinary sensation which our Chinese hosties enjoyed enormously. Apparently, a day out with the gweilos, the Chinese slang word for Westerners, which literally translates into 'foreign devil', was OK! The downside to the swim was that we were caked in salt when we got out, which stung our eyes as we showered it off. But it was well worth the experience.

8. FLYING CIRCUS

'Beautiful Noise'
Neil Diamond

'Your menu choices are chicken or pasta. If we're out of your choice by the time we get to you, don't worry, they all taste the same.'

T he subcontinent was chaotic. The colour, sounds, and smells inundate the senses, and the sheer physicality of the place was another world to me.

BOAC served several destinations there, Delhi, Bombay, Karachi, and Calcutta. Calcutta, with its slums and carts on the road loaded with the dead bodies who had died in the night, was quite possibly the worst stop on the route network. Fortunately, I never went there!

Next on the list came Karachi. Besides the scheduled services, BOAC flew special charters out of Karachi. These flights were bringing over Pakistani immigrants to Britain. Many came from small rural communities where the standard of living was barely above subsistence level. Villages lacked modern conveniences and infrastructure. So, it's not surprising that for many getting on a plane was a daunting, even frightening, experience. Added to that, the technology onboard was a world away from what they knew, especially the loos.

At the best of times, a plane loo is not your run of the mill khazi, certainly not what is to be found in rural Pakistan in 1971! For anyone only familiar with a very rudimentary toilet, things often proved difficult. By the end of a flight, the toilets were somewhere you didn't venture into. The floor would be awash with what should have been safely flushed into the honey tank and crews would be lucky to keep their feet dry! But wait, this was a glamorous occupation. That's not all. It wasn't unheard of for passengers to try setting up BBQs in the middle of the cabin to cook their meals on! I know our food could sometimes be a bit hit and miss, but having a barbie? Maybe on Qantas!

If all that wasn't enough to cope with, crews stayed

at the infamous Karachi Rest House. There was no such thing as an en-suite bedroom, here it was shared bathrooms and you shared your room with the 'roaches. Because of this, the bedrooms were equipped with old fashioned 'Flit' spray guns to kill the little blighters, along with other unwanted wildlife that crawled in under the door. The girls had separate accommodation, known as 'Virgin's Alley', where they had spa facilities. By spa I mean the dubious benefit of an old boy who gave rudimentary pedicures - poolside! Maybe, just maybe, he wasn't as daft as he looked!

And there's no end of stories about the place. One featured a BOAC stewardess being chucked in the swimming pool as she was leaving the hotel for a flight. In the ensuing tussle, the captain ended up in the pool with her! Then there was the tale of a very well-to-do lady swimming one night in the pool, fully clothed in a long evening dress. As she swam around, she was asking anyone in earshot, "*Where's my gin? Where's my gin?*" If it had been Scotch, it would have made more sense!

It wasn't just BOAC that stayed there, crews from across the globe shared the same fate. The best story I heard about the place allegedly involved a Qantas crew. Unlike other airlines, Qantas, operated with all male cabin crews, which may account for this yarn given it has masculine caper written all over it! As the story goes, a Qantas crew put a very sozzled captain to bed after a boys' night out in town. Then they lured a donkey to his room and blocked up the door! The captain must have been utterly bewildered to be woken by a braying and less-than-amused donkey in his room! Now that's one story I pray is true!

My first introduction to the third world filth and squalor that was the subcontinent, where population and poverty live in an unperfect harmony, was when I was rostered to India for the first time in 1971. As I got off the plane, the noise and constant movement hit me. I had arrived in a country in vibrant turmoil. Feral dogs roamed free, even across the airport's runway, and cows meandered around towns and cities as they pleased. Cows would frequently sit in the middle of a road chewing the cud, oblivious to the traffic around them. Indian cows don't fear traffic because of their sacred status – everyone just drives round them or waits for them to get out of the way. What a way to run a country!

One of the first things you realise as a new steward down the routes is that food hygiene in some parts of the world is less than optimal. And India was among the worst places for this with its notrious Delhi belly. Delhi belly was a hazard of the job but it was easily managed, whereas amoebic dysentery, often contracted from eating mulligatawny soup, could be literally deadly. And then there was cholera and typhoid - as I was to discover!

I flew to Bombay pretty frequently. When I was there, crews stayed at the modern Sun and Sand Hotel, located on Juhu Beach, about twelve miles from the city centre. This meant the hotel was well away from the noise and humidity of central Bombay, which is why I never went to see the sights the city had to offer and now I regret never having seen the 'Gateway to India' located on the Bombay waterfront. For the flight deck the hotel was a treat because generally cabin crew got the beach locations and the flight deck guys ended up in the city centre hotels.

On one trip, I was sitting around the Sun & Sands pool with some of the crew chatting to a couple we had flown in the day before; it wasn't uncommon for passengers to stay at the same hotels as we did. Suddenly, one of them sits up and points towards the hotel and says, "*Look at that idiot climbing down the drainpipe*". Sure enough, there was a man climbing down the drainpipe from the first-floor balcony window. The 'idiot' was our captain! When he reached us and introduced himself, the look on the passenger's faces was priceless; this was the person they had entrusted their lives to just the day before! His explanation for the behaviour? He didn't like stairs! Not the most rational, or convincing explanation, I grant you. I imagine the passengers were only too pleased to see us, and him in particular, leave the next day without them.

The hotel was a great location during the day, with the beach home to snake charmers and pole-climbers performing for our amusement. There was also a plethora of urchins and scamps running around trying to beg, steal, or borrow what came their way. But in the evening, it was pretty quiet. One such evening, bored by the prospect of sitting around the hotel, I decided to venture out. This time I wanted to see the infamous Falkland Road area of Bombay known as the Cages. The Cages were old wooden buildings where the ground floor windows had been replaced with metal bars – creating the look of a cage. Hence the name.

Behind these bars sat girls, beckoning to potential customers. It was a truly shocking sight. Girls, as young as eleven or twelve, sat alongside ancient ex-madams, selling themselves for a handful of rupees. This ugly and unpleasant world of prostitution was another of those destinations, like the Bowery in New York, where we went because it was utterly unlike anything else in the world. It certainly wasn't for sex. If that was what you were after, then Bombay was not the place to look for it! Why we wanted to gawk at this human misery and poverty is a complete mystery to me now. In my defense, I didn't go alone; I went with one of our girls, who was equally intrigued to see the place. In both our cases, neither of us had any inkling what we would find there before we set out.

Such was the area's reputation that when the captain heard where we had gone, he sent the navigator after us to fetch us back! As it turned out, we weren't there long enough for him to find us! As soon as we arrived in Falkland Road, our taxi was mobbed. This was because the girl I was with was an attractive, voluptuous white European lass. The excitement in the crowd was palpable. Surrounded on all sides, things quickly reached the point where men started banging on the window to entice us out. No, entice her out. When that didn't work, they started rocking the taxi as happens in riots! To be fair, the taxi driver was more worried than us, so he didn't take much persuasion to make a hasty getaway! The captain's concerns, despite his drainpipe antics, were well founded.

We made it back to the hotel safely enough, followed shortly after by the navigator! We headed for the bar and bought him a few beers for his troubles! Needless to say, I was always a little more wary of where I headed for after that. All part of the rich tapestry that was the learning curve of being long-haul aircrew!

The following morning, perhaps because of what I had seen the evening before, I took pity on a young girl begging on the beach. She had the most beautiful large dark brown eyes that were, sadly, older than her tender years. The thought that she might end up on Falkland Road prompted me to give her money. which was something we were always advised against doing, and here's why.

Our departure from Bombay was early morning, around 6 a.m. On this occasion, as I headed for the bus I was greeted by the young beggar child I'd given money to on the beach - along with all her mates! There were six of them, standing there looking utterly pathetic with their scrawny little hands held out for the odd coin. They had smiles to make your heart melt. I told the rest of the crew about seeing her the previous day and, either out of admiration for her tenacity, or out of a genuine sense of wanting to help, we gave them all the rupees we had. The total amount must have seemed like a fortune to them. As we got on the bus and drove away and they scampered happily back to the beach for another day of begging. There have been many times in my life when I have wondered what became of that little girl. I hope she prospered.

As soon as the bus left the hotel, we were treated to the sight of the 'early morning sitting', where the locals emerge from their homes at first light and head into the fields. All you can see are people's heads appearing and disappearing in the field like apples bobbing in a barrel. This was their early morning visit to the loo! It was an aspect of India that I never found anywhere else in the world, making it little wonder that tummy upsets were commonplace. What do you expect when you use the fields where you grow your crops in as a communal toilet!

The drive to the airport then took us past Juhu airport, which had its own reminder about the dangers of flying! It was here that a Japan Air Lines aircraft had landed, mistaking Juhu for the city's main airport at Santa Cruz – yet another example of planes not landing at the right airport! Because the Juhu runway was very short, once the plane had landed it couldn't stop and ended up coming off the end of the runway close to where the road was. A classic case of pilot error. Although no one died in the accident, seeing the remains of a crashed plane as we set off hardly did much for my confidence, especially when we were positioning to another city in India on one of the local airlines!

Flying within India was something else! Once, we were travelling up to Delhi from Bombay on an Indian Airways Caravelle. Pencil thin, two seats either side of the aisle, the Caravelle was about as different from our aircraft as possible. It held only seventy passengers, and in the rear of the cabin there was a roped off area complete with a live, and pretty smelly, goat. Once in the air, the in-flight service on the two-hour flight proved to be very different to what we provided. With that flight time, we'd serve drinks and a hot meal, along with tea and coffee. For twice the number of passengers! We got a boiled sweet. The goat got better treatment!

****

Back in the day, the Beirut – India/Pakistan – Hong Kong – Tokyo routes were used extensively to smuggle gold by air. And some BOAC stewards were involved at the heart of this illegal trade. India was one of the best markets in the world for contraband gold where the middle classes guzzled gold for jewellery and savings, making it a particularly attractive target for smugglers. Gold was cheaper to buy in places like Beirut, Hong Kong and Macau than it was in India, where street prices were the highest in Asia. This was the foundation of the illicit trade. Criminal gangs in Hong Kong and the Lebanon enlisted seaman and aircrew to work as couriers. Gold was hidden aboard small boats, in ship's cargo holds, in briefcases, and in specially made corsets. Where aircrew were involved, the favoured methods of concealment were the corset and hiding gold tolas under the metal corners of a suitcase lid.

Throughout the 1950s, smugglers became ever more adept in recruiting BOAC crew. For the company, this was a massive concern; with questions even being raised in the House about it.

The involvement of stewards in smuggling activities first came to light in 1951 when two stewards were arrested in Cairo attempting to smuggle gold bars out of the country. The plan had been to deliver the gold to Calcutta. The two men, Bernard Pasche and George Pilbrow, who were on a trip to India, via Cairo, Basra, Karachi, Delhi, and Calcutta, were approached in a Cairo hotel by a man and the plot was hatched. Messrs. Pasche and Pilbrow were detained as they were about to board their plane. When searched, gold to the value of around £11,000 was discovered under their shirts. The pair were court-martialed and sentenced to twelve months' imprisonment. But it wasn't until the mid-fifties that BOAC fully realised the extent to which their crews were involved. It was around this time that one steward decided he could make more money by keeping the gold for himself, rather than handing it over to the gang member in Karachi. He got as far as Beirut on his return trip to London when the gang caught up with him. Somehow, he managed to evade them in Beirut, where he gave them the slip and fled to London, where, after a time, he committed suicide. At least ,that's what the official record has it down as. He could just as well have been murdered. In a separate incident, a former BOAC navigator, Donald Stevens, alleged in a newspaper article, that a BOAC pilot had been murdered in his Calcutta hotel room after announcing to a smuggling gang that he wouldn't work for them any longer. According to Stevens, it *"was made to look like the work of a burglar"*. Two BOAC crew deaths, one that looked like suicide and one that looked like a burglary gone wrong. Makes you wonder.

Throughout the 1950s, and well into the 1960s, BOAC, to their credit, invested heavily in rooting out their criminal element. In one instance, the airline hatched their very own James Bond style counter operation. A security man went under-cover as a steward called 'Roddy'. The idea was to plant ''Roddy' inside the smuggling ring. The plan worked and 'Roddy' was duly recruited. The gang told him he would earn £250 for every trip he made and his first run was to carry gold from Bei-rut to Karachi concealed inside a briefcase. On ar-rival in Karachi, 'Roddy' passed through customs unhindered, thanks to an arrangement with the police, and the delivery was made. At which point, the police pounced and made their arrests.

In another example of the company's attempts to combat the smuggling scourge, one particularly dogged security man, Donald Fish, racked up over 100,000 journey miles in the course of his investi-gations into the racket.

By January 1958, BOAC had gone on the offensive

to eradicate the problem. This was evident when they started sacking staff whom they suspected of having been involved with the gangs, either directly or indirectly. In total, BOAC dismissed forty-nine stewards, two flight deck officers, and a number of ground staff – which gives a clear indication as to the extent of the crew's activities. As part of this house cleaning, BOAC also terminated the contracts of a further twenty-six stewards and one flight engineer. This was solely on the basis of association; they may have worked with a steward who was a smuggler but were innocent of any crime. None of the twenty-seven men were ever prosecuted.

One of those dismissed had been involved in no less than two air crashes while serving with BOAC, so it was a harsh, and very possibly unjust, end to an otherwise distinguished career. Another whose contract was terminated was none other that Len Deighton, later to become one of the UK's top spy writers. At the time, before his writing career had even begun, Deighton worked as a BOAC steward. He always protested his innocence over his dismissal but for him there was an upside. As a steward he had amassed a vast treasure trove of material gathered from places he flew to, material later used to great effect in some of his bestselling novels like 'The Ipcress File', 'Mexico Set', and the 'Berlin Game'! It was the arrest of another steward in 1959 that became one of the most high-profile events of the whole smuggling saga. David Fur-longer, in a counter-smuggling swoop by Indian officials, was caught in Calcutta in possession of illegal gold. Furlonger was on a trip from London, via Beirut, when he was discovered with two gold bars in a belt around his waist, two and a half kilos in weight. He was fined by a Calcutta court £255, but sentenced to goal until the fine was paid. Fur-longer languished in Alipore Central Gaol for six weeks before his wife managed to gather together the money. After finally paying her husband's fine, she said, "*This must have been an isolated case. Now I suppose my husband will be sacked.*" She was wrong on the first count and right on the second! Despite BOAC's efforts, and those of the Indian and Paki-stani authorities, smuggling rings persisted into the 1960s.

In another celebrated case, four BOAC stewards were arrested in Karachi in April 1960. Anthony Wilkinson, Ronald Brooker, Peter Quinn and an-other steward were the first Europeans to be tried by a military court in Karachi, where marital law had been introduced a couple of years previously. The sentences handed down by the court included hard labour, prison terms, and fines.

It has to be said, only a few crew members were smugglers. Some even helped bring the criminals to book by working with the police. In one case, a BOAC national stewardess named Sophie Wong, tipped police off when a smuggler approached her. On a trip to Calcutta, she was introduced to a man in the tea business who suggested she could earn $1500 carrying gold. Once again, the gold would be concealed in a suitcase. Unbeknownst to the smuggler, Wong was engaged to a policeman and she told him of the approach and a sting operation was set in motion.

Wong was given a roster that showed her working on a flight to Calcutta, although this was a decoy. She agreed to meet the gang member in a hotel room, where she was to collect the gold. During the pick-up, the trap was sprung and detectives made the arrest.

By the time I got to India the trade had been stamped out, at least as far as BOAC crew were concerned. Or more accurately, I should say I was never approached or saw any evidence of it. It is highly possible it was still happening because, even now, smuggling remains a pastime aircrew are drawn to. Cases are regularly reported in the news, albeit cases not necessarily related to India and Indian gold. I guess all walks of life have those folk ready to take the risk to make a quick buck or two.

If arriving in India was something of a shock to the system, leaving was the polar opposite. Put simply, a daytime flight leaving Delhi and going east was possibly one of the best flights we did in terms of the view.

From Delhi our flight path would take us on a northern track toward the southern edge of the Himalayas. There, at thirty thousand feet, the view of the massive peaks, especially Mount Everest, was breathtaking. There is simply no better view than that of the world's premier mountain range seen from altitude with the towering snowcapped peaks glinting in the bright morning sunshine! Our route took us north of Hanoi where the wonderful vistas of mountains gave way to landscapes of war. Looking at the ground below, it was hard to believe a war was going on a little way to the south of us, not that far from the track we were on.

It was the Vietnam War and a joint American air and navy task force was busy bombing targets in North Vietnam. Using mighty B52, these were the heaviest bombing raids ever seen since the Second World War. It was a strange feeling to be serving food and drinks while bombs were raining down on North Vietnam a little way to the south of us. Obviously, we were making sure we were keeping well clear of the conflict, but aircraft did stray off course and hostile encounters with unfriendly fighter jets were not unheard of.

It didn't happen often, but it did happen – especially in the Cold War era. As one stewardess, a lady called Pam, recalled, *"I was serving lunch in first class and nearly dropped my Brussel sprouts because I saw a silver MIG, with a red star on the tail, flying parallel to us about two hundred feet from our wingtip. The MIG slipped behind, only to re-appear a couple of minutes later on the other side of the aircraft. It stayed with us for around twenty minutes, then disappeared"*. I grant you, the upsetting of a tray of veg can't constitute a major international incident, but the contact with the jet was real enough.

No such excitement for me; we didn't even have sprouts on the menu!

****

Hong Kong was my favourite destination by far. I loved the place and I reveled in its exotic difference, which began the minute the plane started its descent into Hong Kong's Kai Tak airport. This approach, unlike any others in the world, gave you a foretaste of the truly unique city. Sitting in a geological bowl, Kai Tak had high rise apartment complexes and a mountain to the north-east, and a runway that stuck out into murky waters of Victoria Harbour with water on three sides. The approach we used most often was for Runway 13, not the best omen I grant you. Because of the surrounding terrain, it wasn't possible to make a direct approach over the mountains. Instead, we flew over the city and the guys on the flight deck had to 'aim' for what was called the checkerboard - an orange and white marker painted on the side of the mountain. Once successfully lined up with the checkerboard, they executed a sharp 47° right hand turn at around 600 feet. All this at just under two hundred miles an hour! After making the turn, we then flew at roof top height over the city - and it was alarmingly low. From my seat in the tail, I could clearly see what people had on their washing lines! Television aerials threatened, literally, to remove the undercarriage as we passed overhead only feet above them. Because of the turn and the proximity to the buildings, the approach was dubbed 'Kai-Tak Heart Attack'. After all that, it was then a small matter of getting the plane down on the runway and stopping before ending up in the harbour! I can only imagine what the flight deck must have felt when faced with the approach. To find out, I asked my nephew, a captain with Cathay Pacific, just that. This is how he saw it.

'The final turn (at the checkerboard) needed to be flown manually using only visual references. To say that this approach was unusual, or even outrageous, would be an understatement. The manoeuvre was unprecedented for large jets, so near to the ground, and when low visibility and strong winds were present, the approach could be downright dangerous. So much so that many airlines designated this approach as "captains

only". To make matters worse, the runway
was short and even when things went well, it
focused the mind and quickened the pulse. Kai
Tak approach was not for the faint hearted!'

The approach over the harbour was easier. But, if for any reason, the approach had to be abandoned, you still had to clear those same apartment buildings and mountain and there wasn't much leeway to execute the go-around. It might not have been a very large mountain, but as someone once wrote, '*A little mountain will kill you just as dead as a big one if you fly into it!*' I reckoned the same was true for apartment blocks!

I experienced an abandoned approach in Hong Kong once. We weren't on the 13 approach; we were coming in over the harbour on a very windy day and it was an interesting experience. As we aborted and began to climb, the TV aerials seemed to me to be even closer from this direction! I don't think they were, but I still half expected to see a string of laundry attached to the wheels when we landed!

The landings, despite their challenges, were well worth it. Hong Kong always greeted you with a cacophony of noise, aromas, neon lights, and shirt drenching humidity. The crew hotel was the Hyatt, a high-rise building located off Nathan Road in Tsim Sha Tsui, Kowloon side. Nathan Road was nothing like I had seen before. A 'tat to fab' thoroughfare, running from the Star Ferry Terminal towards the New Territories, it was a manic kaleidoscope of life. The atmosphere was amazing. A non-stop hustle and bustle. Tiny, cramped, shops bursting with goods, street vendors selling live chickens and all manner of birds, and a myriad of small alleys with their bars, nightclubs, massage parlours, and tourist dosshouses.

Amongst all this 'life', there was Sammy's. A visit to Sammy's tailor shop, proper name Sam's, was a must for crew. Sammy's was close to the hotel and was, even then, the undisputed home of the twenty-four hour suit. Nowadays, it's a tourist attraction. Celebrities, kings and queens, and presidents have paid a visit. But back in our day, it was just us aircrew. It was the place to go for a tailor made suit or shirt. And, thanks to a very astute owner, free drinks! The more we drank, the more we bought! I spent many a happy hour sat in Sammy's passing the time away while colleagues had their inside leg measured! I like to think that in some small way, we were a part of creating the legend that is the shop today! For the descendent of a long line of tailors, the idea that we helped create a bit of tailoring history appeals!

After Sammy's, it was off to the Mariner's Club, also close to the hotel, for a beer and a curry. Hard life! The Mariner's Club, as the name suggests, was for sea faring folk but we had membership. Lunch was good and it was cheap. It was here I learned two things about Chinese table manners. The first was that if invited into someone's home for a meal, always leave a little food on the plate from the course you are eating. If you clear the plate, your host will simply bring you more food. And this will go on as long as you don't leave anything; it was the Oriental version of the English 'leaving a bit for Mr. Manners'. In the Chinese version, the table-cloth also needed to show the aftermath of the meal – if you hadn't eaten with sufficient gusto to make a mess you could not have properly enjoyed the meal.

Hong Kong was still a British territory in the early 70s and China had no involvement with the colony. In fact, China was a closed country – not open to outside visitors at all. I knew from press reports that life under Mao's Cultural Revolution was tough. For ten years, millions of lives had been ruined through bloodshed, hunger, and industrial stagnation. But it intrigued me. The fact that it was completely closed to foreigners made it an enigma.

So, one day I took a trip out to the New Territories, located away from Kowloon and Hong Kong Island, to a viewing point at a place called Lok Ma Chau. From here, I could look across the border at the green hills of China. Despite the occasional horrifying press reports to the contrary, I imagined China being like the place depicted in the film, 'The Inn of the Sixth Happiness'. In reality, it was a harsh and brutal place, with a totalitarian regime, incubating inside its own protective cocoon to become a future world superpower. Looking across the border at this closed and secretive place only served to stir the imagination as to what life must be like for anyone living there.

But not all crew wanted to go sightseeing, a lot just headed for the usual haunts on Hong Kong Island. For me, I would head for Stanley Market, situated on the far side of Hong Kong Island in relation to Kowloon. It was an essential trip to do on a layover. I would take the Star Ferry across to Central and then hop into a taxi for the drive down to Stanley, often stopping in Repulse Bay for a drink or lunch.

Stanley was the place to go for under-the-counter fake stuff. It's where most of the Rolex watches, designer bags and branded sunglasses that adorned long-haul crew came from!

By night, it was a visit to the 'Poor Man's Night Club'. Situated on the island, this was a night market famous for its bargain priced electronic and designer knock-offs. So, what you hadn't managed to get in Stanley you could pretty much get there. For those of us with a more adventurous bent, there was another ferry ride to take, this time over to

Macau for a visit to the famous Casino Lisboa.

Known as the Monte Carlo of the Orient, Macau was bigger in those days than Las Vegas. To the Chinese it was a vital outlet for their penchant for gambling. For us it was just another thing to do to pass the time. I remember one visit to the casino well. One of the girls had heard of a fool proof method of winning at blackjack. So, we decided to give it a go. The system was simple. We started with the minimum house bet, and each time we won we placed another minimum bet. When we lost, we doubled the minimum stake we had just played with. If we kept on losing, we kept on doubling. As soon as we won, we went back to the minimum bet amount. The theory was we would get a win eventually and, because the stake kept rising, the winnings would as well. All very well if our pockets were deep enough to survive a run of bad luck!

To start with, we kept winning. Minimum stake after minimum stake. In no time at all, we had built a fair pot of winnings. Happy days! At that point, we should have cashed in - but didn't! When we hit the inevitable losing streak, we were cleaned out in double quick time. I have never seen money disappear so quickly and the speed at which the pot evaporated turned me into a lifelong non-gambler! Although we lost, we still had our return ferry tickets. For those not so lucky, there was always the ferry terminal's pawn shop. Here queues of late-night gamblers, cleaned out at the tables, waited in line to raise the cash for a ticket back to Hong Kong. They would pawn anything they could lay their hands on. Jewellery, wrist-watches, whatever they had. This was the place to go to pick up a real Rolex watch at a bargain price. That said, my daily allowance didn't stretch that far so I never became the proud owner of a genuine Rolex!

If we weren't heading back to London from the Far East our next stop was Australia. At a shade under eleven hours, the flight path took us either down the spine of Malaysia and out across the Timor Sea, or over the Philippines and the Banda and Arafura Seas.

BOAC flew to Perth and Sydney and, on the Sydney route, we made a re-fueling stop in Darwin, which was not the most inviting place on earth. Hot. Humid. Legions of flies. Man-eating salt water crocs. Deadly creepy crawlies. Every imaginable type of venomous snake. These were the inhabitants of Australia's snake capital, along with a few rugged Aussies! It was a dangerous landscape where every living creature was out to kill you. Welcome to Oz! Why Australians want to live there is beyond me!

This was the environment where only stewards on

freighters ended up staying, no crew changes were made on passenger services at Darwin. On one cargo flight, a steward landed there and headed for the hotel, unaware of what was to unfold. Normally, he would expect to be there a day or so at most, only this didn't happen. Day after day he waited for a flight, but no flight arrived. The story goes that he got himself a job in a bar which, combined with the benefit of not having to pay for his hotel room and supported by his daily overseas cash allowance, he was making more than he knew what to do with! After three months, when BOAC finally remembered he was there, he was promptly flown home to explain why he had not been in contact about his plight! For the story to be true, he must have had help from the local station guy. Otherwise, he would have contacted the company about it all. Faced with the same situation, I would have been on the blower for sure to get away from the snakes, et al, as fast as possible! Now, if it had been Hong Kong that would have been a whole different story - I would definately have gone native there!

Wherever we landed in Oz we had to spray the plane with an insecticide to kill any foreign bugs that may have hitched a ride; a process which we also had to do in some parts of Africa and a few other hotspots! To disinfect the aircraft, I would walk through the cabin holding an aerosol spray can as you would an air freshener. Until it had been done, we weren't allowed to open the doors.

Once, on a 707 it went disastrously wrong. As we were taxiing to the terminal, I picked up the can, activated it and set-off down the cabin. Normally, one walk through the cabin and the spray can would be empty. But on this flight, by the time I had walked through the cabin the spray still had plenty left in it. Because the can was a one shot dispensing type there was no way to stop it - it kept on spewing its contents out, hissing like a demented demon. Not entirely sure what to do next, I turned round and came back through the cabin with the spray still going strong. By the time I got back to the rear galley, it still wasn't spent. Unknown to me, some bright spark in maintenance had loaded our little jet with a can we used on Jumbos – which was three times the size we required. By now, mincing up and down the aisle with the can held aloft wasn't an option - the plane resembled the one I had seen on the decompression training video with the entire cabin enveloped in a dense fog. I half expected Boris Karloff to emerge to complete the scene from this Hammer House of Horrors job!

With passengers coughing and spluttering, rubbing their eyes in some distress, I could only chuck the can in the rubbish bin and shut the lid. By the time we got clearance to open the doors, passengers literally groped their way out, zombie style, more or less unable to see through streaming eyes.

And we were in exactly the same boat. Well, plane. One thing was certain, there were no bugs left alive on that flight. Sorry people, but I blame the maintenance guys!

****

My first experience of Christmas in a hot climate was when I arrived in Melbourne in December 1971. With temperatures over 34°C, I completely got why 'I'm Dreaming of a White Christmas' was playing on the radio! It wasn't ironic, it was a wish to feel some cooler air! What I didn't get was seeing Father Christmas dressed in full regalia- it just seemed so out of place with everyone else in shorts and tee-shirts! Christmas carols blasted out from the radio, adding to the sense of surrealism! I particularly remember the radio carrying a news report about a small girl who had been bitten by a spider as she sat on the loo. The spider was the highly venomous Redback Spider, also known as the Australian Black Widow. The little girl ended up in hospital and I spent Christmas, not looking for presents under a tree, but checking for spiders under the toilet seat! All my conceptions about Australia being one giant zoo full of deadly creatures was utterly confirmed!

The crew hotel in Melbourne was nothing to write home about. Nicknamed 'Crossroads', after Central

Television's long running soap, it was not the best. So, it was great to get an invite to a Qantas party to celebrate Christmas. There are lots of stereotypes about Australians and the party proved them right! Very much rooted in the period, this was my first introduction for what passed for the relationship between Aussie men and women! When we got to the party, the room told its own tale! All the men at one end, all the girls at the other. As this was a Qantas party, the girls were friends of the lads, there being no such thing as a Qantas stewardess to invite. After passing the usual opening pleasantries with the guys, I went over to talk to the girls. At this point, I was firmly told this was not the Australian way of doing things! Apparently, the 'sheilas' were just fine on their own! Despite this, and my stereotyping, the evening didn't degenerate into the drunken mess I had imagined all Aussie parties ended up in. Instead, the boys and the girls stayed apart and no-one got that drunk. So much for riotous parties down the routes! Still, the hospitality was genuine - and appreciated!

Routes back from Oz went via Hong Kong or Singapore, and on this occasion it was Singapore. Singapore of the 1970s was an odd place, with a somewhat bizarre culture made up of authoritarian rules and regulations. For one thing, the government banned men for wearing long hair. This was because long hair was associated with

Western hippies, colloquially referred to as long-hairs. To Singaporian government minds, Western hippies represented a drug-fuelled lifestyle. This lifestyle was deemed a corrupting influence on the young and, to be fair, that probably wasn't such a bad call! What was it they said about the 1960s? If you can remember them, then you weren't there. Me? What 1960s?

Men with long hair were fined and, if they worked for the government, sacked! The rule also applied to visitors who could be refused entry on account of their flowing locks or twisted dreadlocks. To get around this, the government offered complimentary haircuts on arrival at the airport which was not a service we ever needed to take up as we were coiffured with a short, respectable, BOAC regulation haircut!

Rock music was also seen as a menace to society with songs 'glorifying' drug use, such as 'Proud Mary' and 'Puff the Magic Dragon', very definitely banned!

Arriving in Singapore. Courtesy Chris Marshall.

Another curious thing were the government posters on billboards all around the city. These posters extolled citizens to refrain from having sex, or more accurately, not to have more than two children per family. Posters with messages like '*Two is enough. The more you have, the more they need*' were everywhere. I swear this is where China got the idea about limiting the size of a family! But this approach to sex, drugs and rock and roll didn't seem to square with what was happening on the streets. I'm referring, of course, to the infamous Bugis Street (pronounced Boo-gie Street) where weird was normal! Bugis Street had a worldwide reputation for its nightly gathering of ladyboys; transvestites whose flamboyant outfits attracted large numbers of curious tourists, sailors, and aircrew!

For my part, I was intrigued to see these Asian

queens strutting their stuff in elaborate dresses and full make-up. They looked fantastic, creating a spectacle like nowhere else in the world that made the street one of Singapore's top haunts. Along with other members of the crew, girls included, I often went there for drinks and the free street show! Occasionally, a ladyboy would try to sit on your lap and pose for a photograph - in return for a fee! Most of the time we just sat and watched them sashay down the street looking for drunk sailors to snare for sex. Ladyboys were always dressed to the nines so, if you didn't know better and were the worse for drink, you could end up with more than you bargained for! The golden rule was, check the size of their Adam's Apple to be sure! The life lessons BOAC was teaching me!

Bugis Street was also famous, or should that be infamous, for the antics of the Royal Navy! Sailors from the British naval base would put on impromptu shows. The show, known as the 'Dance of the Flamers', involved them baring their backsides, inserting a rolled-up copy of the local newspaper therein, which they then set light to. With the newspaper ablaze, they shimmied around with it sticking out of their arses! Little wonder the Navy were thrown out and the base shut down shortly after! Apart from the fact that it was an odd thing to do by anybody's standards, except the Navy's clearly, the fact that the authorities allowed all this to go on whilst men couldn't wear long hair, or listen to 'Puff the Magic Dragon', just didn't make sense to me!

But not long after first going to Singapore the authorities started clamping down on Bugis Street, describing the place as lewd. The clamp down involved visitors and ladyboys being rounded up at gunpoint and bars closed. The strong-arm tactics worked and the place was 'cleaned up' and, just for good measure, the entire street was demolished and a shopping mall erected in its place! Nowadays Bugis Street wouldn't seem at all outrageous, but these were very different times.

Another place crew frequented was Change Alley, which was literally, an alley. Crammed with small shops and makeshift tables, it was the polar opposite of Bugis Street! Hawkers carrying wooden boxes around tried selling us pens, watches, or whatever else they had that day. Street kids shined shoes for a bit of loose change. But the place wasn't just for tourists and aircrew. Locals also packed into the alley, shopping for all manner of things. Humid, congested, and bustling, it was the place we were drawn to like magnets ready to hunt down a bargain and haggle for 'stuff'. BOAC crew luggage tags were popular, but larger items were also bought there. One steward bought an onyx inlaid coffee table, had it wrapped and then proceeded to lug it around the rest of the trip with him as hand baggage! Personally, I couldn't be bothered with the hassle, but it was amusing to watch him struggling across the apron clutching the table and hefting it up the aircraft steps everywhere we stopped!

****

Unlike a lot of crew who claim to have carried loads of celebrities, I only ever carried one 'A' lister, Honor Blackman – aka Pussy Galore in the James Bond film 'Goldfinger'. In the film, Honor Blackman's character leads a team of crack female aviators called 'Pussy Galore's Flying Circus' – employed by 007's infamous billionaire nemesis Goldfinger. I liked the analogy of a flying circus, it seemed highly appropriate to what we were getting up to on a daily basis!

My claim in the celebrity stakes was more mundane, involving an encounter in a Singapore hotel lift. A stewardess and I were on our way up to a room party when Lulu and Maurice Gibb got in the lift. Given the lift wasn't very big, I couldn't have had a closer encounter with not one but two 'A' listers! In that confined area, and being British of course, I said *"Hello"* and, amazingly, Lulu said hello back. Emboldened by this, I jokingly asked them if they fancied coming along to our room party for a drink. Well, if you don't ask you don't get! Imagine waltzing in to the party with them in tow, my bragging rights in the annuls of room party history would be off the scale! To my utter amazement, Lulu said she would love to! Unfortunately hubby, who up to this point hadn't uttered a word, said *"No"*. Not long after this the couple split up so maybe all wasn't well between them as we all stood in that lift? In the brief time it took for the lift to travel between floors, I was left with the impression that Lulu was a really nice down-to-earth type, despite her superstar status. I didn't feel the same could be said for Mr. Gibb!

Inadvertently, I had discovered a valuable career enhancing lesson in that lift in Singapore - the elevator pitch. The elevator pitch are the words you use when you happen to be in a lift with the MD and you are asked something like, "*And what do you do*?" In the time it takes for the lift to travel between floors you have to be able to tell the MD what you do and describe how important your role is to the company's survival! Forty years or so later I think I mastered it - but the process started that day in Singapore!

Lifts were lucky places for me. In another encounter, I ended up in a lift in Macau with a Miss World contestant – accompanied by two very large minders. As in Singapore, it was all a bit close, but this time I kept my mouth shut! Not that a Miss World contestant was such a big deal. This was because I occasionally flew with a former Miss Jamaica who worked as a BOAC stewardess - and she was a real stunner. Our paths crossed on Caribbean routes and, if being drop dead gorgeous wasn't enough, she was one of the nicest stewardesses I ever met. So, being in a cramped galley with her was no hardship whatsoever! I think I may even have been a little bit smitten!

****

Another place on our Far East route map was Rangoon. Although I only went there once I shall never forget what happened there. We were making a forty-five-minute transit stop and, after we were back in the air, I went to prep for the evening drinks service. But there was a problem, I seemed to have left Rangoon without a bar box! Where the box should have been, I only had an empty container. My firt thought was that it must have been loaded in the forward galley, as sometimes happened if space was tight down the back. But it wasn't there and I had obviously left the wretched thing behind.

Despite our training, mistakes did happen - it's only human nature. But to lose an entire bar was an epic failure! Not to mention the cost to me when the ABD form got handed in at the end of the trip! No amount of tinkering with 'broken bottles' on all the next sectors would cover this little lot!

'Your drink, sir'. Not how it looked that evening in
Rangoon! (BA Speedbird Heritage Centre)

Fortunately, I did have the box with the duty-free
bottles in it, so we could still offer a drinks service
of sorts but it meant passengers wouldn't be getting duty-free goods this flight.

How had I messed up so badly?

A check of the paperwork showed I'd signed for the
missing box; which only served to make matters
worse. I'd signed for a full bar and taken delivery of
an empty box! How could I have been so gullible?
The loaders must have seen me coming from the
airport's outer marker! But then it dawned on me
how it had happened. I was definitely responsible,
but at least there were extenuating circumstances.

During the transit we'd had an incident that

caused a fair bit of disruption in the cabin. Pandemonium would be a better word. A snake had found its way into the cabin when the catering was being loaded. It must have been on the caterer's truck and decided on taking a holiday. I saw it as it slithered around the rear bulkhead heading out of the galley. As it disappeared behind the last row of passenger seats the rumpus began. There were passengers scrambling to get out of their seats, with passengers and bags going in all directions! With the snake somewhere under the seats, it made for a scene from the theatre of the absurd. It didn't help that, when asked to describe the reptile, I was a bit vague. A snake is a snake, for pity's sake. It wasn't as if I had the time to study it in any detail! But the question remained, was it harmless or was it deadly?

After a bit, one of the loaders, a braver chap than me, managed to trap the snake using one of the aircraft's blankets and successfully remove it from the plane. It was only then we discovered the snake was poisonous but not lethally so. Amid all this confusion, I had obviously signed for the bar without checking and the loaders, otherwise engaged on snake retrieval, had forgotten to load it. Fortunately for me, a call back to Rangoon established they had the box and it was still full. Thank heavens for honest loaders! It would have been far more common, in a lot of places we flew to, for someone to have had the contents away! If that had happened, I would have faced a difficult conversation with the 'thimble ladies' on my return to London – having to fork out the loss from my wages!

****

Somewhere else I flew to regularly was Thailand which, at the time, had little by way of an international profile and a great deal of downtown Bangkok, the capital, was distinctly seedy. But things were starting to change in the early 1970s with new hotels opening in the hope of attracting the long-haul tourist.

Whenever I was in Bangkok, I would do my usual thing and go off exploring the local sights, such as the 'Temple of the Golden Mountain' and the 'Temple of the Emerald Buddha'. With their saffron-robed monks and a soundtrack of melodic chanting filling the air I found the temples fascinating and they made an impression on me that lingered.

I also enjoyed getting out and about in the city using the longis to explore the place. Situated along the Chao Phraya River, the longis are waterways that gave the city a different feeling from any other, with the exception of Venice – hence why it was nicknamed the 'Venice of the East'. I would often grab a water taxi, cheap as chips to use, and set off among the back waters in order to see for myself the way the local folk lived. I was never disappointed, there was always something new to see and discover – like an evening shadow theatre with their haunting images projected on a white screen. I had no idea what the stories were about but they held the audience in bouts of rapt attention and corresponding howls of laughter! For me, this was far more enjoyable, not to mention healthier, than seeking out the multitude of flesh pots Bangkok had to offer - as so many crew did!

I was told a tale (apocryphal story or not) about a first steward, who readily admitted enjoying the company of ladies from one such fleshpot. This poor unfortunate came away from one encounter with more than he'd bargained for. The rash appeared on the flight home and, as the flight progressed, the itching intensified. Keen to rid himself of this memento he decided on a rudimentary home remedy, albeit a drastic one. He shoved a load of Ajax, which we carried on the aircraft, down his trousers! Ajax was a 1960s scouring powder, a strong bleach in powder form that was definitely not formulated for human medicinal use - although the artist Francis Bacon is reputed to have used Vim, the American equivalent, as a substitute for toothpaste. But let's face it, powdered bleach and a man's private parts should never mix! By the time the flight landed he had to go to hospital for treatment to the resulting skin burns in his nether regions. A salutary lesson for one and all!

Little wonder I prefered temples to knocking shops!

9. EAT YOUR HEART OUT, PHILEAS FOGG!

'I'd Like to Teach the World to Sing'

The New Seekers

'We'll be dimming the lights to enhance the appearance of the cabin crew.'

On average, a steward could expect an even spread of trips to destinations across all four continents, with a round-the-world trip thrown in for good measure about every six months. But I only ever did one round-the-world trip. Not only that, I never got to fly to many of the really interesting places we served, such as Tokyo, Moscow, Lima, or Anchorage. I clearly couldn't be spared for these trips as my presence across the Atlantic and down Africa way was utterly indispensible!

My one and only time going right around the world was the best trip I ever had, bar none. Our route took us to Bahrain - Singapore – Sydney – Fiji – Honolulu - Los Angeles - New York – London. This was usually a three-week roster but I started by positioning out to Singapore, missing out the scheduled layovers in both the Gulf and India. Instead of the usual twenty-one days, I did it in sixteen - so in some respects I never did enjoy the whole round-the-word expereince so many crew did. But I did do part of the trip as a first-class passenger - which was not normally part of the deal!

I left Heathrow with a stewardess called Christine, who was joining the same crew as me. After boarding, we found our seats in Economy and settled in for the eighteen-hour flight. As we were pushing back from the gate the chief steward invited us to move to first-class – not just for the first sector but all the way to Singapore! So, there I was, just twenty-one, travelling BOAC first-class in the company of a very attractive blond! At that moment, I didn't miss the world of accountancy! Come to think of it, I never missed the world of accountancy, ever!

Christine and I hit it off straight away, chatting all

the way to Bahrain. Here we picked up a fresh crew who, unbeknownst to them or us, were the crew we were joining in Singapore. Why we didn't hook up with them in Bahrain I have no idea - such were the vagaries of crew scheduling!

Not long after leaving Bahrain, we decided a bit of shut eye was called for and Chris puts her head on my shoulder and snuggles down for a kip. The first-class steward, going about his duties, cast envious eyes on us. He later confessed he was a bit miffed that a bloke as young as me could afford first class - with an attractive girlfriend thrown in for good measure! Little did he know. I wasn't rich and she wasn't my girlfriend! I wasn't even his rank!

During our rest period in Singapore, Chris and I went our separate ways, only joining up again when we met up with the crew on the bus out to the airport. The first steward, who we now knew as Victor, did one of those comedy double takes when he first saw us clamber aboard the crew bus. Still, it broke the ice when he told us what he had thought of us on the way out! From that moment, the three of us got on famously.

In Sydney, our crew hotel was out at Bondi Beach. Back in the 70's, Bondi was a popular spot with families seeking the sun – not a backpacker or tattoo parlour in sight! As our hotel was self-catering apartments with large and spacious rooms, Vic and I decided to throw a room party for the rest of the crew. The centrepiece of the evening was to be Vic's specialty – vodka sours. Everywhere he went down the routes he would take his 'special case'. The briefcase contained everything needed to rustle up a vodka sour, except for the egg. Inevitably, we nicknamed him, Vodka Vic. The sours were lethally good.

By all accounts, the party was a pretty standard affair with everyone getting quietly sozzled as the hours ticked by. But it did have one stand-out comedy moment. In the early hours, Chris had fallen asleep on the bed and, in our drunken stupor, we thought it would be a wheeze to treat her to a gentle massage, compliments of the bed's built-in massage function. Once we had rustled up the necessary coins, and managed to feed them into the machine, not easy when you are three sheets to the wind, the bed came alive. As it started to undulate and vibrate, Goldilocks definitely responded to the movement with gyrations that left little to the imagination! Of course, she knew nothing about any of it, but we kept on reminding her about it for the rest of the trip. If we'd had smart phones back then, it would have been a YouTube sensation!

BOAC's round-the-world service returned to the UK from Australia across the Pacific. The first stop, after a short four and a half hour flight, was Fiji. It was here that I enjoyed one the best days of my life on an idyllic and uninhabited island in the middle of the Pacific Ocean.

Intent on making the most of the trip we chartered a boat to go and explore the island. We had found a couple of locals, dressed in traditional Fijian skirts, who were only too happy to take us out on their sloop in return for suitable recompense! I have never seen such huge men. Bulldozers in shorts would be an apt description! In that moment, I found a new level of respect for our international rugby players! I cannot imagine what it must feel like to have these guys bearing down on you intent on flatteniing you to the floor. That said, I now know these people to be gentle giants, so I'll forgive them the skirt thing!

The sloop was magnificent. Its sleek white hull and matching white sails looked amazing against the deep blue of the sea and sky. With long white clouds drifting across the sky, it was picture perfect as we chased across the sea, heeled over with sails full of wind. The crew not only caught lunch as we sailed, they entertained us as well. We were treated to an impromptu jam session played on guitar, comb and paper and a pebble in a beer can! Given their limited instruments, they managed to make a great sound.

On arrival at the island, the boat guys built a fire

on the beach and started knocking coconuts off the trees along the edge of the beach. We all tried our hand at this, simply lobbing sticks into the tree and coconuts rained down. This was the life I had signed up for!

While lunch was cooking, we went swimming. Snorkeling around in the lagoon, I came across what looked like a shoal of barracuda. Given their reputation, I gave them a wide berth but later discovered they were nothing more than harmless needlefish. I preferred the idea of saying I had swum with deadly barracudas!

We ate lunch on the beach; the fish we had caught was roasted over an open fire, washed down with copious cans of local beer. It felt more like we were shipwrecked castaways than aircrew on a day's outing – all very Robinson Crusoe!

Later that same day and after dark back at the Mocambo Lodge, the crew hotel, we gathered in the hotel grounds to listen to a group of locals singing 'Pokarekare Ana'. Although not a traditional Fijian song, this World War 1 Maori love song captivated me and I have enjoyed Maori music ever since. Maoris had come through Fiji on their migration to New Zealand - 'the land of the long white cloud'. Against a backdrop of a large banyan tree and a clear moonlight sky, it was easy to imagine the time when those long sea canoes first pulled up on the island's pristine beaches. A magical end to a magical day. I didn't know then, but some fifty years later I would return to Fiji where I was made an honorary Fijian chief!

We departed Fiji for Honolulu the next day. Shortly after boarding, our chief steward gave us stewards a present as a memento of our time in Fiji. It was a small ethnic folk figure carved out of local wood, but with a surprise up its sleeve. Or rather, between its legs! As I picked it up, the legs dropped down from the body and a huge phallus leapt out – and up! Apparently, it was the Fijian version of the Fillipino barrel man – where the same thing happens. All to do with fertility rites! At the start of a working day, I appreciated the humour, if not the innuendo, and the fact that the chief steward was clearly having as good a trip as the rest of us!

There was no shortage of colourful characters masquerading as chief stewards. One legend, nicknamed Half Pint, was a master prankster. One of his more elaborate japes involved unwinding the inside of a tampon and attaching this to the peak of a first officer's hat before landing, a mickey take on the 'scrambled egg' a captain wore on his hat. On at least one occasion, he stitched up the sleeves of a first officer's uniform jacket as well! Half Pint had many sayings attributed to him. I particularly like the one he had when showing first class passengers to their seat. As they sat down, he would say quietly, "*Tickle your arse with a feather, madam*". If challenged about what he had said, his urbane response was, "*Particularly nasty weather, madam*". If it wasn't Half Pint who said this, it could have been any one of the larger-than-life-characters who flew as chief stewards over the years with nicknames like Officer Dibble or Dirty Bertie - to name but two!

One Polish chief steward I flew with had his own unique way of making sure beverages were served hot. He'd stick his finger into the tea or coffee pot to test the temperature! If he couldn't keep his finger in the pot for more than a couple of seconds, it was good to go! I'm not sure passengers would have approved if they knew his fingers had been in there! I suspect he may have learnt this from the 'Half Pint School for Stewards'! If a passenger ever dared to complain that their food wasn't hot on one of Half Pint's flights, he would storm into the galley holding one finger up to the offending steward saying, "*Use your effing fermometer!*"

One of the most colourful, and camp, chief stewards I flew with was Arnold. A flamboyant queen, he was an accomplished concert pianist - and a great steward. I first encountered him as I was positioning out with the rest of the crew to our first night stop, Frankfurt. It was the start of a twenty-one day Sydney terminator. Why we were positioning to Frankfurt and not working from

London I can't recall but we were travelling first class. Picture this. I am standing in first class chatting to one of the crew when Arnold walks up behind me and a hand snakes around my waist before attempting to slide down the front of my trousers. *"Hello heart. I'm your chief steward"*, was all I heard. Needless to say, for the rest of that trip I was extremely wary of him! To be fair, it worked out to my advantage. Every time Arnold came into the galley the girls would huddle round me to protect me! My very own Charlie's Angels! I needn't have worried though; in the end I came to like Arnold. He was a gentle, kind, and sensitive soul living with a broken heart. On the crew bus in Sydney, sitting next to me, he told me about the love of his life who had sadly died on active service with the British Army in Aden. It was something he had never got over. So many years later, he was still moved to tears. After that trip, the next time I saw Arnold was in Jo'burg. I was down by the pool when he appears on his bedroom balcony wearing a fluffy pink dressing gown. As if in a box at the Royal Albert Hall he shouts down at me, *"Heart, darling, I'm here. I'm yours. Forever."* I just curled up on my sunlounger hoping people would think it wasn't me he was addressing! After that, whenever I ran into him, he would repeat the same mantra. Needless to say, I never gave him any encouragement - he didn't need it!

The flight to Honolulu was six hours twenty

minutes and involved us crossing the International Date Line. This is an imaginary line drawn down the middle of the Pacific Ocean used for world time keeping. From Fiji we crossed the line travelling east, so we subtracted a day. Going the other way, we had to add a day. All this did little to help alleviate my permanent state of jet-lag! It was possible on some flights, because the Date Line dog legs around Samoa and Kiribati, to cross the line twice in the same day. Or should that be today and yesterday? Still not sure.

After a long night sector, our approach into Hawaii took us across the east side of the island over Pearl Harbour. As you flew over the harbour you could see the wreck of the USS Arizona, a battleship that was torpedoed and sunk by the Japanese in the infamous attack on the harbour during World War II. To this day, there are still eight hundred sailors entombed in the hull but flying over it there was no sign it was a war grave. Te hull is now a covered memorial, with the USS Missouri, another World War II battleship, lying alongside it as its guardship.

Hawaii, or more accurately the island of Honolulu, was a big disappointment to me. Aloha shirts, tacky cocktail bars, and wobbly dashboard hula dolls wasn't my idea of Hawaii. What I had expected was the island portrayed in the Elvis Presley film, 'Blue Hawaii'. The idyll of pristine sand and turquoise blue water, where island girls danced in grass skirts to the sound of guitars, as depicted in the film, was, in reality, a tacky urban playground awash with tourist tat. My disappointment in the place was compounded and confirmed when I got up one morning to enjoy the view of the world famous Waikiki Beach from my hotel balcony. I saw city corporation dumper trucks emptying lorry loads of sand on the beach which, without this daily infusion, would have simply been washed away. Given the great time we had in Fiji, a true island idyll, the comparison between the two places couldn't have been more striking!

From Honolulu the next leg was a five-and-a-half-hour flight to California, classified as an internal US flight. Because of this, we weren't allowed to charge passengers for drinks. Consequently, passengers were always in a good mood after imbibing the free booze, which we helped foster by serving Mai Tai cocktails – our trans-pacific specialty. These were served in the same type of beaker we used for the Rum Swizzles in the Caribbean, only this time printed with the details of the Mai Tai.

We landed in LA just after sunset, making this one of the best approaches on the timetable. The first time I saw it, I was mesmerised by the myriad of thousands of fairy lights creating a spectacular star-studded carpet that stretched as far as the eye could see. I've never tired of seeing any city from the air at night, but LA was on another level.

On LA stop overs crews generally headed out to the beach at Santa Monica, where Route 66 finally runs out of land, or they went to see the pavement stars on Hollywood's Walk of Fame. The first time I went to LA, I went to Disneyland! And it's not as lame as it sounds.

The Los Angeles Disneyland was the first one ever opened, and the only one built by the man himself, Walt Disney. The Magic Kingdom had recently opened in Florida, but Disneyland was still like an eighth wonder of the world at the time. Crews were drawn to it like bees drawn to honey. The best ride was the 'Pirates of the Caribbean', which I loved. I also loved 'It's a Small World'. What can I say, I have eclectic tastes! Little wonder then we headed there instead of the other iconic sights!

The last leg of our circumnavigation of the globe took us to New York, then back to London via Prestwick. As we boarded the plane for the flight to New York the inbound crew told us what had happened on that sector. A couple, with ambitions to join the fabled mile-high club, had started to get amorous, with one thing leading to another. Before long they were at in their seats in full view of the other passengers! In typically English style, the chief steward asked them to refrain! They weren't, apparently, in listening mode. Their minds, and hands, were on other matters! Faced with this public display of affection the only thing the chief steward could do was to throw a blanket over them with the instruction to keep the noise down. *"What else was I supposed to do?"* he said, with a mischievous grin on his face. I guess it was the climax of the flight!

All this was long forgotten by the time we had stopped off in New York and were on our way back across the Atlantic on yet another red eye transatlantic crossing. This flight went via Prestwick, where we were going to carry out one of the first automated landings for a BOAC plane on a scheduled service - one full of fare paying punters! Automated landings, where the aircraft lands itself, was a new concept for commercial airliners back then. Although we were breaking new ground, BOAC had been beaten to the post by BEA. They may have been the 'Back Each Afternoon' airline, but they carried out the first auto landing at Heathrow six years earlier aboard a Trident-1 inbound from Paris. So, in the early 1970s we were playing catch-up by equipping our VC10s with the autoland system.

As we flew the approach into Prestwick it was clear this was not a run of the mill landing. From my seat between the engines, the way the engines were hunting, constantly powering up and throttling back, told me that much. Despite the rather disconcerting way the engines were behaving we kissed the runway in one of the smoothest landings I ever experienced! It was a bit special to be a part of that VC10 crew making a little bit of aviation history. The aircraft, G-ASGC, is now on display at Duxford as part of the British Airliners Collection and it is the only BOAC plane I worked on to have survived the scrapyard.

Despite our success at Prestwick, we rarely used the system on landing. This was because most airports at the time didn't have the ground equipment the system needed! Low visibility problems on landing remained an issue for years, with routine use of autoland a long way distant in the future.

After all the fun of the trip we landed back at Heathrow later that morning heralding the end of my first, and only, complete circumnavigation of the globe! Eat your heart out, Phileas Fogg. I'd done mine in less than twenty-one days!

****

One of the hazards of the job was a trip to the rummage shed. The rummage shed at Heathrow was a Customs facility where crew could end up for a random baggage check. After a long flight, the last thing I needed was the hassle of the dumb-fool questions and someone rooting around in my dirty washing! For obvious reasons, the place was not a crew favourite. But it has to be admitted some crew did pilfer items from the aircraft and hotels, so it was a necessary evil. In one case, a steward's home was raided and found stacked to the rafters with contraband – cash, booze, drugs, and a plethora of stuff liberated from hotels!

We were taken to the shed in a Custom's mini-bus. On one infamous occasion, as the bus headed away from the plane and across the apron, small packages could be seen being thrown out of the windows! On examination, these were found to contain a white powder which, predictably, caused much consternation with Customs who immediately assumed it was drugs. The answer, as it turned out, was a tad more prosaic. The packets contained nothing worse than washing powder one of the stewardesses kept for doing her smalls down the routes. What I can't reconcile with this story is if it was only washing powder why chuck it out of the window? Maybe it was the crew's sense of mischief at work. Whatever the truth of it, I bet they were taken to the cleaners when they reached the shed!

A trip to the shed always made me sit up and take notice. This was because I hadn't been flying long before I dreamt up a lucrative scheme, a nice little earner that relied on circumventing UK import duties! The scheme involved diamond rings and the idea was built on the premise that I could buy diamonds in Hong Kong far cheaper than in the UK because they were duty-free. So, I would buy a solitaire diamond engagement ring from a High Street jeweller as cheap as possible with a large clasp and a small stone. I then took the ring out to Hong Kong to have the stone replaced with a larger one. This way, I could more than quadruple the value of the ring when I sold it back in the UK. To get around having to pay the tax on the newly installed diamond when I returned to London I'd ask one of the girls to wear it until we got safely back to crew reporting. As the ring bore a UK hallmark, Customs never questioned its origin. If it had been bought abroad there would be no UK hallmark! All I had to do was first ensure the girls were wearing the ring before Customs arrived and make sure I got it back from them at Crew Reporting! I cannot remember how many girls I was engaged to during my flying career!

If we weren't taken off to the rummage shed, we were cleared by Customs on the plane. Even this involved a few dodges – but this time aided and abetted by the Customs guys themselves. As crew, we had a duty-free allowance which applied to full bottles of booze. On anything over and above our allowances, we had to pay duty. To get round this we used the 'part-bottle' ploy. Part bottles, ones that had been opened and some of the booze consumed, didn't attract duty so we would break the seal and offer the Customs guys a 'drink'. They didn't actually take a drink as they were on duty, instead the measure went into a hip flask. Voila, as we now had a part-bottle duty wasn't payable! The great thing about this bit of skullduggery was we could more or less take as many bottles through as we could carry. Cheers!

10. DEAD RECKONING

'Spirit in the Sky'
Norman Greenbaum

*'We'll be landing as soon as we get
closer to the ground.'*

Before the introduction of the 747, BOAC moved most of its cargo around the world on a small fleet of Boeing 707 freighter aircraft. The cargo carried was an eclectic mix. Live sharks, gold bullion, exotic birds, monkeys, horses, crocodiles, rhinos, even elephants, made up a manifesto menagerie. If it was certified to go by air and it would fit in a container, cage, or box, we would fly it! Even King Tutankhamun got in on the act when he went on a world tour aboard BOAC in the 1970s!

Working on freighters was always interesting. One steward told me about the time he looked through the main freight door and came face to face with an adult lion! Then there was the steward who looked into a crate, through a hole that had been torn in it by its occupant, and was promptly punched on the nose by a baby gorilla! It might have been a baby but it still broke his nose!

Freighters may have carried some exotic cargo, but they also carried the best named bit of aviation kit ever - a 'fish muff'. When I first heard the term, I thought lady-parts! Easy mistake to make! As it turned out, a 'fish muff' is an insulated container for carrying tropical fish on cargo flights!

Of course, on freighters we didn't have any passengers to worry about. My job was to feed the piranhas, as pilots and engineers were known by some of us! (Pilots also went under the collective name of Nigel, for reasons I know not!) More used to dishing out meals to over a hundred people per flight, dealing with the flight deck was a piece of cake.

When it came to my first freighter trip, I was looking forward to it and expecting an interesting cargo. But it wasn't to be; the cargo was just a load of run of the mill goods, nothing exciting, nothing alive! The excitement came from the flight itself due to a series of events that are forever indelibly etched on my mind.

Our route was London to New York, with stops on the way in both Manchester and Prestwick and then out over the Atlantic on a northerly track. Before departure from London, I was in the galley organising myself when I saw the captain coming up the aircraft steps. He had an artificial leg. My first thought was how had he passed the medical? My second thought was could he fly the plane with only one good leg. It was my first experience of seeing a pilot, let alone a captain, who was less than fully able bodied but I consoled myself when I remembered the stories that had filled my head as a boy where Douglas Bader, played by Kenneth Moore in the epic movie 'Reach for The Skies', flew his Spitfire in the Battle of Britain with two artificial legs! I needn't have been concerned, despite a gammy leg, this particular captain could fly perfectly well! In the end it wasn't his flying skills that were in question but his somewhat maverick approach to safety and regulations. Which was probably why he was flying cargo and not passengers. Either way, it was a potent mix just waiting for some mishap to happen!

After departure from London, we stopped off in Manchester to pick up more cargo. For the take-off from Manchester, the captain invited me on to the flight deck but the only problem was there was no-where for me to sit because we had a check pilot on board (checking up on the navigator) who was occupying the jump seat. This didn't faze the captain. He told me to stand with my back against the flight deck door and hold tight. On no account, he said, was I to fall forward should we abort the take-off as to do so would have meant ending up straddled across the instrument panel between the pilots across vital flight controls! That's what I am talking about - a maverick approach to the rules!

As we thundered down the runway, standing on the flight deck was just the best feeling. The sensation of speed and movement as the plane took off was amazing. It felt like I was flying and was certainly better than my usual seat near the tail! I was allowed to repeat the process when we landed at Prestwick and it was just as exhilarating!

From Prestwick we headed out across the Atlantic, flying a track that took us south of Greenland. As we didn't have the benefit of GPS navigation in those days, pilots navigated using a combination of dead reckoning (using a map and a compass), doppler navigation (a system for calculating the aircraft's ground speed and drift from the planned route), and celestial navigation (a process of astronomical observation that involved shoving a bubble sextant into a roof port to take sightings of the stars, sun, or planets). Navigators could also call

Ocean Station Ships (weather ships) on the radio to confirm the plane's position. You can't beat having to ask for directions mid-Atlantic! You can imagine the conversation, *"Excuse me chaps, but are we ...."*. Using these methods, aircraft were able to keep to within five to ten nautical miles on the planned route. Not exactly precise by modern standards, but it got us there and back every time without the use of onboard computers, fancy laptops, or an array of other electronic wizardry!

As I had little to do having served the flight deck their breakfast, the flight engineer showed me how to trim the fuel tanks. This involved pumping fuel from the wing tanks into the main tank housed in the fuselage, allowing the balance of the plane's centre of gravity to be adjusted. This process enabled the plane to maintain straight and level flight, a task I was to undertake for real when the flight engineer went for a loo break - leaving me in control of the panel! This definitely wasn't covered on training and was another prime example of the rule book being discarded!

While I was sitting at the flight engineer's panel I glanced out of the first officer's side window and spotted what looked like land covered in snow and ice. I asked the first officer where it was and he told me it was an ice flow that had drifted south. He didn't look. After another ten minutes or so I saw more snow and ice. And this time I could clearly see mountains! On an ice flow? I told the first officer what I had seen but he said it couldn't be as we were nowhere near land. I begged to differ. I may have been a lowly second steward playing with the fuel, but I grew up in Switzerland and know a mountain when I see one! He still didn't look! It was a couple of minutes later when the first officer finally peered out the window and saw what I was on about. We were definitely flying over land! To be precise, it was Greenland and we should have been nowhere near the place as our planned route was some miles to the south of the coast. Something had clearly gone awry in the navigation department!

As you would expect, there was some concern on the flight deck at this unexpected turn of events. To cut a long story short, it turned out we'd made a navigation error earlier in the flight and altered course based on an erroneous sun sighting. We were now heading in the general direction of the North Pole, not flying east to west toward Newfoundland! I guess that meant the navigator failed his check flight!

After correcting the mistake we resumed course for New York, which we only just made as we were flying on fumes with our fuel tanks pretty well drained to zero by the time we started our final approach. What was this about our aircraft always running on low fuel levels? Part of the culture, I guess.

What would have happened if I hadn't noticed anything? The error might well have been discovered, but it would have been too late given the state of our fuel on landing and we would have been faced with an unscheduled landing somewhere in the frozen north. Now that would have been an adventure!

The next day we were all back at JFK for the return flight but the events of the previous day meant the flight deck were in a more regulation frame of mind, so no standing for me on take-off or landing this time!

One of the things I liked about working on freighters was the time we had onboard before we closed the doors and pushed back from the gate. With only the flight deck to feed, it took no time at all to check I had all the catering uplifts I needed so I had time to look at what was happening on the apron as loaders, refuellers, dispatchers, and assorted ground staff scurried around the place. It was a bit like watching a ballet, albeit with a fairly butch looking cast!

As a steward, when I closed the door for departure, I was acutely aware that it represented the culmination of a lot of effort, by a lot of people, to get the plane away on time. And it wasn't only the folk

I could see hurrying around the apron; there was an army of people working toward the same goal throughout the company right across the globe. People like long-suffering check-in staff, engineers vital to our survival, reservations and sales teams who kept the passengers coming with money to pay my wages, cooks, bean counters, bus drivers, dispatchers, and the bloke who drove the 'honey-wagon' full of toilet waste. Then there were an assortment of office bods engaged in all manner of activity, from purchasing food and drink to liasing with government departments, all of whom played their part in this aviation ballet. That's why, despite all the pranks and larking about, I did my best to do the job to the highest possible standard. Not only did I owe it to all those unsung heroes, but I also owed it to myself.

By and large, I believe I succeeded.

11. WHAT CAN POSSIBLY GO WRONG?

'All Right Now'

Free

*'Ladies and Gentlemen. Please remain in your seats
with your seatbelts fastened whilst the captain
taxis what's left of the plane to the gate.'*

One of the perks of the job was staff travel,
which allowed us to fly on a standby
ticket for ten percent of the economy class
fare. As flying standby didn't guarantee you a seat,
it meant you might not get on the flight to begin
with, or you could end up being off-loaded somewhere down the route. Apart from that, what

could possibly go wrong?

On one staff travel trip to Mauritius I found out the answer to that question! The return flight to London went via Cairo so I thought it would be a great idea to break the journey there and see the Pyramids at Gisa. As a steward, I had access to manuals on the aircraft that set out the visa requirements for every country we served, and Egypt was one of those countries. Having checked what was needed I was confident I had it covered. Yet, as soon as I stepped off the plane in the dead of night, I quickly discovered otherwise!

On arrival at passport control I was told my entry visa was 'not in order'. According to the officer, I had to pay extra to get the 'right' visa. Knowing this was nonsense (I had the visa I needed) I decided to stand my ground and refused to pay the baksheesh. Any money I paid to them was only going straight into their back pocket and this annoyed me. So I refused! Almost immediately, my passport suddenly developed 'irregularities' and I was taken off to an 'interview room'.

At this point, I started to become concerned. The immigration guy's attitude was pretty threatening. As I didn't speak any Egyptian and they didn't speak more than a few rudimentary words of English communication was difficult. After a couple of hours of being 'interviewed', and spat at, I figured out I was under arrest of sorts. During this time the exchange that passed for a conversation saw matters escalate. It had all started out about a 'visa issue', i.e I wouldn't pay the bribe, which had then turned into a 'passport problem' and now, out of nowhere, they decided I might be an Israeli terrorist trying to infiltrate the country in the dead of night! From the sublime to the ridiculous – Egyptian style!

Apparently, I was trying to 'sneak' into the country at two o'clock in the morning with 'false' documents. And my nose didn't help! In profile, and with my vaguely olive skin, I could pass for an Israeli! Of course, it was all total nonsense but by five in the morning the 'joke' was wearing thin and the inside of an Egyptian prison beckoned. I even tried giving them the money they had originally wanted but that provoked the accusation I was trying to bribe them! Heaven forfend, them being bribed!

Finally, after my many demands that they call the BOAC Station Manager to verify my bone-fides, they did so. By now it was six o'clock and I was free to leave, but as a deportee! My passport was marked to prevent me entering the country in the future, the 'price' to be paid to avoid a formal arrest and trial! With the centre pages of my passport covered in hand written Arabic, I was then frog marched across a sun blistered tarmac to the waiting aircraft, escorted on both sides by policeman carrying AK-47 rifles.

Ah, the joys of staff travel!

After the Cairo encounter, you would think I couldn't end up in another pickle on a staff trip, but I did. This time it was Beirut, in the summer of 1973.

Middle East Airlines were offering BOAC staff free return tickets to Beirut which was an offer not to be missed! What I had missed was the 'why'. We were being offered the freebies because MEA's load factors were very low because tourists had stopped going there! That should have rung an alarm bell or two, but the lure of free tickets was too much to refuse so off I went for a long weekend in the Lebanon. How jet set can you get?

The flight out on their ageing 707 was unremarkable. It wasn't until I was on the way into the city from the airport that it became clear this wasn't going to be the relaxing break I'd imagined. The tensions I had sensed on earlier working trips there had well and truly surfaced. The gunfire that had started in 1970 now occurred with alarming regularity. No wonder, MEA offered free tickets to anyone daft enough to venture out there.

Earlier that year, Israelis jets had attacked the

Shatila refugee camp, close to Beirut's airport, along with a number of other targets in Lebanon. Lebanese government forces had also attacked Palestinian guerillas camps in Lebanon with planes and tanks, and armed members of the Popular Front for the Liberation of Palestine had 'arrested' two Lebanese soldiers which resulted in a major gunfight when the army turned up at the gates of Shatila. Shatila was an unfortunate place to live, clearly. The Lebanese Government, having previously taken in the Palestinian refugees and given them safe harbour in camps like Shatila, now found itself trying to prevent the refugees from taking Lebanon over for themselves and turning it into a new Palestinian homeland. This conflict, played out regularly on the streets of Beirut, was to end up in a full-scale civil war just two years later and I was there to witness the early days of it all. Some place for a weekend break!

The city was not a good place to be. Shops, banks and restaurants were shut. Many of the residential areas deserted. Tanks on every corner. Trigger happy soldiers patrolled the street. It was kind of cool, in an exhilarating way.

One image from the weekend left a huge impression. It was that of a woman begging on the street, cradling a dead child in her arms. For a lad from an English middle-class background raised in the Home Counties, it was a shocking sight. For the woman it was an act of desperation. She had little choice. Begging with a child in her arms gave her a good chance of someone taking pity on the child and giving her money. Without the child, she had nothing with which to pull at the heart strings. Faced with this dilemma, she grimly held on to the child when she should have let the little one be laid to rest.

Because of the situation, prices for food, taxis, and goods were way higher than I had expected, or budgeted for! Consequently, I ran out of money pretty fast. As I didn't have a credit card in those days, this presented a bit of a problem. With the banks closed, I had to improvise! After asking around, I ended up cashing a UK bank cheque with a shady character in the hotel's laundry! It was a strange experience writing out an English cheque in the bowels of a Beirut hotel, but it did the trick and I left with enough cash to get me through the rest of my stay!

As time went by, it became increasingly obvious the city was going to hell in a handcart. Having solved my cash crisis another, more serious one, presented itself. MEA suddenly closed their flights to staff ticket holders in order to make more seats available to the hoardes of people now looking to get out of Beirut! And they could give me no in-dication of when staff would be able to get on a flight! Unless I could sort something out, I was going to have to find the chap in the laundry again and blag some more cash!

Just as they do in the movies, I decided the best thing for me to do was to head to the airport and try my luck there. When I got there the place was in chaos. It appeared as if the whole of Beirut was trying to leave at the same time. The concourse was packed with people jostling at the various airline desks trying to get a seat on any available flight out. Men with briefcases, women with children in hand, tourists, porters, all manner of airport staff, and me.

I did have one thing going for me – I was BOAC aircrew. So, I ventured into the melee in search of the local station manager. When I found him, he told me he had two flights due that day but staff would be a very low priority. It was anyone's guess when the next aircraft would be through after that, he helpfully pointed out. As staying wasn't an attractive option, I resolved to get on one of those planes! I failed with the first one and almost failed with the second because I was on an MEA freebie ticket, not even a BOAC staff ticket! But then I got lucky.

A free seat magically became available on the flight in first class no less, and my situation was transformed. I was on way way home thanks to the captain making me a priority on account of how I was aircrew! I never did get a chance to thank either the station manager or captain so if they are reading this - thanks. Talk about all's well that ends well!

The very next morning, safely back at home, I read that the proverbial had hit the fan in Beirut and there was widespread fighting across the city. BOAC had suspended all flights there.

Whatever else can be said for the weekend, it definitely had a taste of adventure about it!

12. ELEPHANT TASK

'Cum on Feel the Noize'

Slade

'For those of you wondering about the weather at our destination, Honolulu is reporting sunny skies and temperatures of 86 degrees. Unfortunately, our destination is reporting 27 degrees below zero and snow!'

Called by some the 'Queen of the Skies', although many would argue this title belongs to the VC10, the Boeing 747 was more commonly known to the public as the 'Jumbo Jet'. Carrying three hundred and sixty-two passengers, it made long-haul travel affordable for many people for the very first time. In the same way the Golden Age of Flying had ended in the 1960s, the

Jumbo heralded the beginning of the end for the 'mini fleet'.

Marketed with the strap line, 'More sitting room in the sky', the plane had lots of space making it an immediate hit with passengers. Compared to the cramped layout of the 707 and VC10, two aisles replaced a single aisle and there was an upstairs! Interestingly, this wasn't the first double decker aircraft BOAC had ever operated; the first was the Boeing Stratocruiser in the 1950s, complete with a downstairs bar!

Stairs to upper lounge on 747. (BA Speedbird Heritage Centre)

The 747 slashed travel times to Australia. A VC10 or 707 took around thirty-four hours to complete the trip with five stops en-route, whereas the 747 did it in something like twenty-four hours with just two stops. This may have been great for passengers, but for crew it represented less time down the routes and a far more humdrum routine – all work and less play!

BOAC took delivery of its first 747 the year before I joined. As the number of 747's in the fleet increased it was a sure fire bet I would get transferred to them - which, of course, happened. At the time, the Board of Trade restricted the number of planes we could work on at any one time to just three types, which meant I had to leave the small jets behind as the 747 would have been aircraft type number four for me. Many crews managed to dodge the draft to stay on the VC 10 and 707 fleet, but I wasn't one of the lucky ones. Had I been, I would have undoubtedly continued flying for longer. When the fateful day came for me to join the 747 fleet, I entered an entirely different and far less attractive world.

No longer was I part of a crew of six, I was now one of fourteen: a cabin service director, a purser, one senior steward, an 'A' bird, two first stewards, two second stewards, three stewardesses ('B', 'C', and 'D'), and four 'bar tarts' - stewardesses responsible for the bars! Bar tarts were known by a host of other names, 'trolley dollies', 'air fairies', 'truck sluts', and 'wagon dragons' - to name but a few! Gone were the intimate and small cabins with their serene air of calm and quiet I had enjoyed. One hundred and forty passengers had become three hundred and fifty plus – and the noise levels in the cabin reflected that increase! It was a bit of a zoo by comparison!

Boeing 747 economy-class cabin. (BA Speedbird Heritage Centre)

To work on the 747 I had to complete a conversion course, so it was back to Cranebank for five-days. Part of this included a visit to the plane to see the cavernous monster for ourselves. Luckily, the galley had a few familiar items of equipment. The ovens and water boilers were the same as I was used to although we did have one wizard bit of new kit, a microwave oven! Microwaves weren't on the market for domestic use at the time - they didn't arrive on the High Street until a couple of years later. So, we got to use them ahead of most people - and we also got to break them ahead of most people. As we were to discover, in the middle of a busy meal service, it was easy to forget to remove a spoon or fork before hitting the 'Start' button. Remembering the metal bit didn't immediately come to mind when using this piece of newfangled equipment! But despite the revolutionary new microwave, we still hadn't got rid of the dreaded hot cup. It was still there, spitting its vengeance over us at every opportunity!

Another new bit of kit on the aircraft was the in-flight entertainment system. This boasted ceiling mounted projectors and screens hidden behind decorative bulkhead panels. The days of pulling screens down from the ceiling for them to flap merrily away in the middle of the aisle were well and truly behind us. All we now had to do was flip the panels round and there was the screen. This may sound quaint today with tv screens in the back of every seat, but it was cutting edge stuff to us!

If it was cutting edge for me, then to some folk it was something to defy their comprehension. One such person was a wonderful old lady called Mrs. Walker, whom my mother looked after. Mrs. Walker's mother was Lady Nancy Rootes, married to Sir Reginald of Rootes car fame. The very same company that built the Hillman that the Iranian Paykan was copied on. It amused Reggie when I described the traffic in Tehran as being all his fault!

Mrs. Walker loved hearing about the exploits of my latest trip, and I would spend hours chatting with her. To her, the fact that we had four 'cinema' screens on the plane was more than she could contemplate. In her day, she flew from Croydon Airport on Imperial Airways flights to Paris. The seats were wicker and the cabins fitted out with spittoons! There was no such thing as in-flight catering. They would make it across the Channel and then land in a field near Le Touquet where the steward (this being pre-1934 when there were no stewardesses on aircraft) would lay out rugs and baskets on the grass and hold a picnic for passengers. Then it was back on board for the last leg to Paris! To Mrs. Walker, a 747 with over three hundred passengers flying nonstop for eight to ten hours, complete with talking pictures was nothing short of a miracle. Thankfully, we had no spittoons!

My job was dramatically different to what I did on the smaller jets. I was no longer in charge of the galley or bar - that was now the realm of the girls. My work area was in the back of economy and all I had to do was serve meals and drinks from the trolley and smile, but there wasn't a lot of fun to be had running endless meal trays and cups of tea up and down the aisle.

As with any aviation activity, it did have its moments. Such as when the cabin filled with smoke on take-off out of Heathrow on yet another North Atlantic trip! When I saw the smoke my first thought was an engine fire. My second thought went straight back to Whiskey Echo's fateful departure from Heathrow. I immediately called the chief steward's door position on the intercom and reported what I could see. By now, the smoke was becoming thicker by the minute. Meanwhile, we continued on our departure climb out as though nothing was amiss.

After checking with the flight deck, the chief steward called back to say there was nothing to worry about, it was just engine exhaust fumes leaking into the cabin ventilation system. Known as a fume event, it didn't seem to be a big deal to him. Didn't he know people die from carbon monoxide fumes? To be fair, the captain was quick to reassure passengers that there was nothing to worry about. Nothing to worry about? He should have been sitting where I was! A plane full of smoke, no matter what fancy name you give it, can't be right. The smoke did eventually clear, but not until after passengers and crew were left with streaming eyes and spluttering coughs. And I was no where near an insecticide cannister at the time! Still, it was only a fume event! Thankfully, this only happened to me once in my entire time flying, which conclusively proved to me that what happened that day was anything but normal - despite the captain's silky words of reassurance! But it wasn't only smoke incidents I remember from the 747.

From time to time, we had to deal with suicidal passengers. Aviophobia, otherwise known as the fear of flying, is all too real for many people so it was not unusual to come across passengers nervous about being on a plane. This manifested itself in a number of different ways. There were the quiet passengers, sitting as small as they could in their seat, looking terrified and wringing the life out of their companion's hand. Then there were the passengers clutching at sick bags as if that were their only hope of survival. And there were the vocal ones who were truly terrified and who made their fear known to one and all. One such woman sticks in the mind.

It was on a Toronto - London service, at the end of a five day Atlantic 'shuttle' trip, when this particular incident unfolded. It was a foul night outside with a freezing cold temperature, driving rain, and an Arctic wind blowing off the polar ice cap. We were delayed at the gate due to an engine problem which, despite the weather conditions, the ground engineers remedied in just under forty-five-minutes. While they were freezing their buts off outside fixing the glitch, our own drama was unfolding in the comfort of our warm and dry cabin. A well-dressed woman in her thirties had become very distraught. Afraid of flying, she was in a total panic about the plane's impending departure and had lost her nerve, her cool, and her reason. Such was the level of her distress that she got up to go to the toilet proclaiming loudly that she was going to commit suicide. Now, I am not sure if that's the way suicidal people behave, telling others about their intentions, but given her obvious distress she was taken seriously and persuaded by the chief steward to resume her seat – in return for a promise the plane would not leave until she was calmer. But she had a crazed look in her eyes I have never seen in anyone again; I guess it was sheer terror at the prospect of the flight. Given the state she was in, the chief steward sought the assistance of the airport's paramedics. However, their appearance only served to make matters worse and, despite their best efforts to calm her down, she remained adamant about her intentions. By now, our engine was fixed and we were ready to depart so something had to be done. When it became clear the plane would be departing, the woman was convinced by the medics to leave the flight. After the usual further delay to locate and remove her luggage from the hold we were well over two hours behind schedule and still had a full Atlantic night sector stretching out ahead of us. Who said the life of an air steward was dull or easy?

In fact, it was rarely dull. There was always the element of the unexpected that sprang out of a clear blue sky, such as severe turbulence!

Travelling across the Atlantic as frequently as we did, it was normal to encounter the odd bump or two by way of turbulence but, because of its size, the Jumbo was a fairly stable aircraft compared to what I was used to. But I never expected what happened on one of my early 747 trips.

We were in the middle of the meal service high above the Atlantic Ocean when, without warning, the turbulence began. The right wing dipped violently and the plane 'slid' sideways and downwards on its wing tip. We dropped over five hundred feet before the wing levelled and we shot back up. The suddenness and the violence of the move caught us completely unawares. But that wasn't the end of it with the sequence repeating itself over and over again with me being tossed around the cabin like a rag doll. It was as though I had stepped onto a roller coaster. In this situation, the immediate priority was to get the trolleys back in from the aisles and stowed away in the galley. Leaving them out there and strapping myself in was not an option. To say that getting the trolleys back down the aisle was tricky is the understatement of the century. When we, myself and the stewardess, finally wrestled them into the galley, things became even more difficult.

Without the aisle seats to stop their sideways movement, the trolleys were overcoming our best efforts to get them safely into their stowage. At one point I was desperately hanging on to a trolley as it dragged me from one side of the galley to the other. Every time the wing dropped, I went flying - if you pardon the pun - only stopping when the trolley smashed heavily into the door on either side. Such was the violence of it all, I remember hoping the door wouldn't burst open! Rationally I knew it couldn't, but in those circumstances my mind ditched logical thought. Eventually, I did manage to get it stowed away and get myself strapped in. After we landed, the captain explained over the PA that we couldn't have climbed or descended to get out of the turbulence as we had planes above and below us all the way across. The one below was clearly nearer at times than those above us - five hundred foot nearer to be precise! The next day the bruises on my arms and legs were testament to the severity of that turbulence.

Despite her size, the 747 was a surprisingly nimble aircraft and pilots would say she was easy and forgiving to fly. Take the plane's versatile abilities on landing. For instance, when 'heavies' like a 747 land they use reverse thrust to slow down as do all jet airliners. Right? Well, not always. I found this out one day on a landing into Bombay. Our first officer had a unique party piece, landing a 747 without applying any reverse thrust and, for reasons I now forget, he could only do this at Bombay. It was a weird experience. The absence of noise and vibration normally experienced on landing was unsettling. As we touched down, at the slowest speed possible, we sailed on down the runway with hardly a sound. The usual racket from the engines and the shaking that comes when re-

verse thrust is deployed just wasn't there. To slow the plane down the first officer only used ground brakes and spoilers, allowing the fully loaded monster to glide almost silently down the runway before serenely turning on to the taxiway. It was very impressive!

The plane was also responsive in the air, as I found out on one approach to Hong Kong. We were inbound from Australia and our approach was over the harbour, not the checkerboard. As it happened, weather conditions that day were not exactly balmy. On the tail end of a tropical cyclone, the winds were making the job of lining up with the runway's centre line extremely tricky. To complicate matters, the airport's instrument landing system (ILS), a system that ensures you stay clear of trees, surrounding hills, buildings, etc., wasn't working due to maintenance being carried out on it. To make the landing, the pilots had to rely on their skill of flying a visual only approach. To be fair to them, a lot of pilots flew this way even when ILS was available – but not in these weather conditions! As if all that were not enough, when the plane reached decision height, the height at which the pilot must commit to the landing or abort it, some of the critical instrumentation on the flight deck failed. In theory, as the flight systems had duplicate sets of instruments for both pilots this shouldn't have been a problem – but both sets failed at the same time. So much for redundancy theory!

On the harbour approach, when an aircraft needs to abort a landing, the challenge was to avoid flying straight into Lion Rock, a hillside that lay dead ahead and bang on the climb out from the runway. To avoid such unpleasantness pilots had to apply full power and immediately bank steeply away to avoid the hill. It took us three attempts to land this day before finally nailling it!

The first go-around was interesting. As on the checkerboard approach, the skyscrapers and hillside seemed just as close as they did on landing. When we went round a second time, I was less keen on the ride as the skyscrapers seemed to be getting closer! As we tried the third time, I was fully expecting us to give up and head for Manilla, our divert airport. But we didn't, and we made the landing stick, albeit in a pretty robust manner. The guys up front slamming down onto the runwaay to make absolutely sure we were well and truly down. The landing made me think of the story of the little old lady getting off a plane after a hard landing and then asking the crew *"Have we landed or did we just crash"*.

****

The one thing we never had to deal with, irrespective of the plane we were on, were passengers dying. This was because no one officially dies on a flight. If a passenger happened to inconveniently shuffle off their mortal coil at thirty thousand feet, death was never pronounced during the flight. This was done when the poor soul reached a hospital. But, of course, whatever way you look at it, people did die on us.

I only had one person drop dead in front of me, although of course he wasn't officially dead! It happened in the middle of the evening meal service. As I came out of one of the central galleys carrying a pot of coffee, a man coming down the aisle towards me went down like a sack of potatoes. It was clear something was seriously wrong. My aviation medicine skills were about to be put to the test, and the stakes were high. I dumped the coffee back in the galley and went to attend to the passenger. Fortunately for me, as I reached the man a woman came running down the aisle saying she was a nurse and immediately assumed command of the situation - which I had no problem with. If the plane was on fire and we had to evacuate passengers, I would not defer to a passenger. But this was different. In reality my medical skills were, to all intent and purpose, non-existent.

The meal service was suspended while the guy on the floor was attended to and the obligatory PA call for a 'doctor on board' was made. Fortunately, we did have one on the flight. As he and the nurse looked after the casualty, we set about moving passengers to clear a space on the back row for him. After moving the unfortunate gentleman there, the doctor spent a lot of time administering to him but it was clear early on this was a lost cause. The man was dead. All we could do was cover him in a blanket, leaving his head showing. He looked, for all the world, to be just another passenger asleep. To have covered his head would not have been a reassuring sight for all the other passengers, especially those in nearby seats! After landing, the ambulance crew came and took him off to hospital, where he 'died'. Looking back on the incident, there was nothing anyone could have done to save him. He was past help, even before he hit the floor.

****

Taking off from Nairobi in a 747 was more exciting than most places we departed from. At an altitude of five thousand five hundred feet above sea level, getting airborne was a bit of a struggle as the plane needed every inch of runway to get airborne. So much so, we couldn't take-off with a full load of both passengers and cargo. We had to go with less passengers and a full cargo load, or vice versa. For all their attributes, our 747s were not the most powerful of aircraft with woefully under powered engines. The early BOAC 747s had a lounge on the upper deck, not because the company wanted to provide top notch facilities, but because we couldn't use the space for passenger seating because this would have made the aircraft too heavy to get off the ground! Eventually, the engine power issues were resolved and the lounge did become another cabin with seats in it. At Nairobi, in particular, just when it looked like we would run out of runway the plane would finally claw its way into the sky. But only just! Sitting down by the rear door, the runway stop lights and perimeter fence were closer than a Hong Kong washing line! Every time I took off from that runway, I lifted my backside off the seat as we cleared the fence! Of course, it didn't help but it was impossible not to react that way because the fence seemed awfully close! I guess it was alright for the guys at the pointy end, but down the back it was a near tail strike every time!

The strangest trip I ever did on a 747 was an overnight flight from Nairobi back to London, complete with the mandatory backside lift from me on take-off! As we only had forty-odd passengers onboard I looked forward to an easy night. Or so I thought. But I hadn't factored in the group of Mexican seamen and their parrot!

BOAC flew a lot of sailors around-the-world, both on charter flights and scheduled services and Nairobi was a key destination where merchant sailors joined or left their ship at the nearby port of Mombasa. This particular night a group of Mexican seamen were on the flight to London, where they would make an onward connection to Mexico City. But unbeknownst to us cabin crew they had a parrot in a cage hidden in a cabin bag, despite the fact that animals and pets were not allowed to travel in the aircraft's cabin. Assorted livestock, cats and dogs, snakes and spiders, terrapins and tropical fish, etc. travelled in the forward hold and not in the cabin with passengers! How the parrot made it into the cabin in the first place is a mystery. However, given the lack of security in those days in places like Africa, and the power of the ubiquitous backhander, I suppose it wasn't all that surprising! For our part, we were completely unaware we had a stowaway until about an hour into the flight when the parrot got out of the cage!

Of course, the inevitable happened. Free of its cage, the delighted bird merrily proceeded to squawk and flap its way around the front section of the economy cabin. Free as a bird, so to speak. And much to the consternation of those sitting in that area as not many people are keen on being dive bombed by low flying birds, let alone in the confines of an aircraft cabin.

For my part, the sight of a parrot putting on an aerobatic display at thirty thousand feet pursued by inebriated sailors was knee-buckling stuff.

Unlike the parrot in the Monty Python sketch, our bird definitely wasn't dead, deceased, resting, stunned, or shagged out after a long squawk. It was very much alive! It was a scene straight out of a West End farce or a Hitchcock movie! With the parrot flapping round, passengers ducking to avoid an unwanted encounter, and Mexicans clambering all over the seats trying to recapture the damn thing, chaos reigned. You couldn't make it up. Ever the professional, I just stood there, surveying the chaos, with tears of laughter cascading down my cheeks! After a bit, the Mexicans managed to grab the parrot and shove it back in its cage. By now, the Mexicans were in high spirits so they decided to celebrate the mayhem with a raucous sing song, accompanied by a couple of guitars. The impromptu cabaret, which would normally have been frowned upon for the noise, was better than the parrot's antics! I have absolutely no idea how the purser explained the shenanigans in his flight report, but I expect the rubbish bin was full to bursting with customer forms!

Before landing it was decided a landing drink was in order after such an eventful trip. The teapot duly arrived and we all grabbed a glass, chatting happily behind the drawn galley curtains. Completely unaware of where we were on the approach, we were all still standing around in the galley when we landed. Oops! We should, of course, have been strapped in our seats prepared to evacuate the plane, if necessary. Instead, we were supping champagne! Somehow, it seemed a perfectly normal and fitting end to a totally crazy night!

By complete contrast, on another Nairobi trip I saw how the 'other half', the first class cabin crew, lived. As a second steward on the 747 my work-place was in economy, but on one Nairobi - Jo'burg leg I got 'promoted' to work in first-class and asked to look after the upstairs cocktail lounge on the small upper deck, accessed via a spiral staircase leading up from the first-class cabin.

As I only had one customer, I wasn't exactly busy so I spent most of my time looking out of the window at the African landscape rolling below us. This was the life! Far easier than fighting the scrum down the back!

I didn't realise it at the time, but that short spell in the upstairs lounge was the moment the seed was sown to quit flying. It made me realise just how much I disliked working in 'cattle class' and that I had no intention of suffering doing that job long enough to be promoted to work in first class!

Looking back on it, I have often wondered if that was a good decision. Perhaps I should have hung in down the back until I was promoted. Had I done so, not ony would I have worked in the genteel

environent of first class, but I would also have become eligible to fly on Concorde when that entered
service.

Who knows, I may even have made a career as an
air steward, rising to the rank of Chief Steward!

C'est la vie!

14. THE FINAL TOUCHDOWN

'The Last Time'

Rolling Stones

'We have begun our descent. If London is not your planned destination for today, it soon will be.'

A few years went by before I decided to hand in my notice and return to a 'jet-lag free' civvy street. The fact that I cannot remember a single detail about my last flight as aircrew is telling! Nevertheless, during my time with BOAC I had flown thousands of miles and served thousands of meals. I had been to five continents and visited twenty-six countries – something I would never have done had I stuck with the relentless excitement accountancy had to offer!

I hadn't crashed or been hijacked. In fact, no BOAC aircraft was involved in an accident or incident during my time flying with them. I'd never experienced any serious technical malfunction in flight and nothing ever fell off at thirty thousand feet! I hadn't suffered any exploding engines, cabin depressurisations, or wheels up landings - not so much as a burst tyre.

Despite my misgivings about working on the 747, I wouldn't have missed it for the world. Although I didn't realise it at the time, I was going to miss the life. I would miss jetting off to explore far flung places, lounging around sun drenched hotels, and generally being a provider of food and good times for one and all! But most of all, I would miss the camaraderie of the crew and the sense of adventure that came with the job. But all good things come to an end, and I only have myself to blame if that was a bit premature!

Life after BOAC didn't get off to the best of starts. In the same month I stopped flying, BOAC ceased to exist when it merged with BEA to become British Airways. We had both come to the end of an era. And I too, nearly ceased to exist! A few days after leaving, I found myself fighting for my life in St Anne's Hospital, Tottenham. I had contracted typhoid down the routes in my last days of flying, which I most likely picked up in India. I had inadvertently swopped a reasonably glamorous life travelling the world for a tiny sterile hospital cubicle in an isolation ward with only a view of the hospital's incinerator chimney! Life inside the cubicle was bleak, to say the least.

The ward comprised several of these boxes where most, but not all, contained very ill patients! Between us patients we boasted a whole range of deadly diseases - smallpox, rabies, cholera, and typhoid. The one exception was an old lady across the passage from my cubicle. She didn't have an infectious disease, I guess she was there because of the way she made her presence felt. Night and day, she would shout and scream at the top of her voice. I figured they felt we were too sick to be bothered by her noise which is why she was in there in the first place. As I drifted in and out of consciousness in my first days of incarceration, I thought I had died and gone to hell!

It was in this mad house that I learned of what I had contracted. The doctor breezed into my cubicle one day when I was finally compos mentis and announced he had some good and bad news. I opted for the good news first.

"The good news", he said, *"is that we now know what's*

wrong with you. You have typhoid".

"And the bad?", I feebly enquired.

"Ah yes, well, there's no cure".

Mortuary humour, I guess. But it wasn't just the doctors who enjoyed a bit of a laugh at the patient's expense. When I was eventually allowed to eat solid food, the orderly, a massive Caribbean woman with an equally massive sunny disposition, set up my bed tray for lunch. After days and days on liquids the sight of a knife, fork and spoon were uplifting. When the food arrived, this Caribbean angel placed the plate on my tray and removed the lid with a proud flourish. My heart sank. Instead of a plate of real food, all I had was a small bowl with a couple of mouthfuls of cold custard in it. *"You won't be needing these, then,"* she said with a big grin on her face as she removed the knife and fork. Talk about building a fella's hopes up!

About three weeks after that, by now well on the road to recovery, the mortuary humour was back in the room, this time courtesy of the hospital porter.

Through the large inside windows that ran along the side of my cubicle, I saw the porter wheeling what looked like a body down the corridor. As he passed by, he winked and said, "*Your lucky, this is how most of them leave here!*" The fact that it wasn't me on that trolley was thanks to those vaccinations I'd had with BOAC; they literally saved my life.

My new role after BOAC was working for Cunard Leisure as Area Sales Manager for their Caribbean hotels, which meant I was always out in the Caribbean flying on the same BOAC aircraft I had worked on but now sporting British Airways livery and I was now the one being waited on by stewards and stewardess, many of whom I knew!

On account of the frequency of my trips to the Caribbean, and because of a random conversation at a trade delegation bash in London with someone I was later told was a 'civil servant', I was approached by a representative of a UK Government trade quango and asked to visit Dominica on their behalf. Clearly, I had come up in the world from being a lowly galley slave! As the story goes, the Dominicans hoped Cunard might make the island a port of call for their cruise ships and open a hotel on the island as part of their drive to improve the island's dirt-poor economy. My brief was to see if there was merit in the idea. My qualifications for this? None. I was only being roped in because I was in that neck of the woods anyway! What anyone failed to mention was that the island was in the middle of a violent uprising at the time!

Blissfully unaware of the situation, I duly arrived on Dominica aboard a LIAT Airways island hopper plane from St Lucia. As I disembarked, a huge black guy stepped forward and introduced himself as Charles, my driver and close protection officer. As we left the airport via a side gate, excused the usual immigration formalities, I felt like a VIP! Walking toward the car, I noticed Charles was wearing a firearm so I asked him why the gun. Was it normal for him to carry it? He explained that political activists were attacking the island's economy in order to topple the government and their methods were extreme. They had recently killed a Canadian farmer after torching his farmhouse! The extremists were attacking people important to the economy and, as Charles explained, I would be a valuable target for them! *"But I won't use it* (the gun)," he said, *"I'll use this".* And with that he reached into the car and lifted a huge machete off the front seat. *"They will not like this,"* he added with a grin. I think I preferred the gun!

That night, I had dinner at my hotel with members of the island's Cabinet, which turned out to be a very a convivial affair despite the presence in the room of several 'heavies' – armed to the teeth with an assortment of weaponry. I sat next to the Prime Minister's wife, a very tall and elegant woman. Opposite me was the Prime Minister, Premier John. Premier John, in total contrast to his wife, was a short and rather unassuming individual – more

Dudley Moore than imposing statesman! During dinner I was asked if I would like to try the local delicacy, which I accepted on account of it being the diplomatic thing to do. It was toad! Apparently, there are only two types of edible toad in the world and one of these lived high up in the island's hills! It tasted like chicken, but I think if I knew in advance that it was toad it wouldn't have been so enjoyable!

After dinner, when the dignitaries and bodyguards had left, I shared a nightcap with the hotel's owner and, without their looming presence, I suddenly felt vulnerable. The fact the hotel owner was also a Canadian running an important business made me doubly nervous. Even his offer to let me spend the night with one of his two girlfriends didn't make me feel any safer! Had I accepted the invitation it would absolutely have taken my mind off the situation!

My hotel room opened out onto a beautiful black lava beach, which twinkled in the moonlight. But instead of the room having patio-style doors opening on to the beach, it boasted only a wrought iron framework. Devoid of any glass, the frame also had a convenient space between the wall for the odd guerilla to slip through in order to slit your throat in the dead of night! Perhaps I shouldn't have been so hasty to turn down the offer of the girl! Certain I would be murdered in my bed, I slept little that night! In the event, the only thing to come in and out of the room were bats, divebombing me as I lay there watching the 'window'!

I was collected early the next day by the gun totting Charles and spent the day visiting the site where the proposed port was to be built and seeing Roseau, the capital, for myself. It soon became obvious the island's infrastructure, with or without a port, was not up to the job. Facilities, such as they were, were extremely basic and it was not at all clear to me how they could deal with an influx of cruise passengers and hotel guests. That aside, the political situation ruled it out and my report back to London said exactly that. Yet that didn't stop the island's newspaper reporting that 'Dominica is to be recommended for inclusion in the visits of Cunard ships to the Caribbean'. Really? It goes to show you shouldn't believe everything you read in the newspapers!

Years later it occurred to me that if Cunard had wanted to assess the situation for themsleves, they would have done it themselves, using someone who knew something about shipping! My report was far more likely to have informed my 'civil servant' friend on the state of the island and, given my dubious credentials, I felt the whole affair had more than a whiff of trickery about it!

As for Premier John he resigned shortly after my

trip following further violence and unrest on the island. He later carried out a coup to regain power, but ended up in goal for twelve years when the coup failed! I was once again keeping dubious company - just as I had, on occasion, when flying!

Now, looking back on those days across a span of more than forty years, it's easy to remember events in a nostalgic way - through the prism of heavily rose coloured spectacles. But the reality was different and, as the years have rolled by, life-back then looks increasingly old-fashioned. For a start, all BOAC planes had four engines - it was the norm. Today, there are very few four-engine fuel guzzling passenger planes flying, and for those still in service their days are well and truly numbered.

The Golden Age of Flying may have come to an end by the 1970s, but it was still an Age of Adventure, free from the constraints of political correctness, not to mention health and safety dictats. It was also an age of limited technology, tech being in its infancy at this point in history. True, the available tech had put men on the moon and created supersonic passenger flight in the form of Concorde, but every smart phone on the planet today has more processing power than any plane I ever worked on. Pilots had navigators and flight engineers to help fly the plane, collectively finding their way around the globe by checking the position of the sun and stars and scribbling on a map! There was no GPS or electronic flight bags - just good old-fashioned brain power.

Today's inflight entertainment systems, with their digital chips and processors, don't need a pair of tights to keep them running! Crossword books, much favoured by BOAC passengers, are almost a thing of the past. Now you ponder cryptic clues displayed on the seat back screen in front of you – along with almost everything else the Internet has to offer.

Interestingly, the process for preparing and serving food on aircraft has changed little over the years. When I see a galley nowadays, I still recognise the same type of equipment we used all those years ago.

What is beyond dispute is the fact we had some of the most colourful characters ever to work in the airline business and all in an atmosphere that was, to say the least, chauvinist and politically incorrect. But boys and girls alike had a fun time and amid all the pranks and high jinks, we delivered a level of service to our passengers that even now those folk recall with great affection.

In the end, I guess we must have got something right! Now, where did I leave those rose coloured spectacles?

AFTERWORD

Cocktail Recipes

C hampagne Cocktail. First, run some lemon juice around the rim of a champagne glass and then dip the glass in the sugar to coat the rim. Place a sugar cube into the glass and drip two drops of Angostura Bitters on to it. Pour brandy to cover the top of the sugar cube, and then fill with champagne. Simple, retro, lethal!

R um Swizzler. Place 1 measure dark rum, ½ measure of lime juice, ½ measure of sugar syrup, 1 dash Angostura Bitters, and crushed ice into a suitable beaker of cocktail shaker. Shake to mix. Garnish with orange slice and a cherry.

M ai Tai. Made with 2oz white rum, 1 oz lime juice, ½ teaspoon Orange Curacas, and crushed ice. Garnish with spear of pineapple, mint, and orchid. Stir before serving.

"I'D LIKE TO THANK.."

My thanks go to all those who have helped in the writing of this book. Thanks to BA Speedbird Heritage Centre for their support and to Dan Clark and Chris Marshall for the use of their photographs, to Ian Turner, airline captain, for his insight into landing at Hong Kong's Kai Tak airport, and to all those online ex-colleagues, particularly Steve Frampton, whose recollections and support have greatly assisted my ageing memory! Thanks also to Peter Moore as I shamelessly pinched his idea of adding a soundtrack to each chapter, as he did in his book, 'The Wrong Way Home.'

Thanks must go to the various anonymous sources I used for the airline quotes cited at the start of each chapter; they are randomly taken from aviation sources and not BOAC archives!

Finally, thanks go to my wife, Susan, and daughter-in-law, Lucy, for their invaluable help in the production of the book.

Printed in Great Britain
by Amazon